The Great Commission

❖ ❖ ❖

The Solution...

The Great Commission

❖ ❖ ❖

The Solution . . .

ISBN 978-1-59684-474-2

Edited by Bill George

Published by Pathway Press
1080 Montgomery Avenue
Cleveland, Tennessee 37311

Printed in the United States of America

Supplementary material to this book is at
http://www.greatcommission.cc

For information about the Church of God, visit the Web site:
http://www.churchofgod.org

For my friend

Floyd D. Carey

An innovative, competent, consistent creator
of church-developing, life-impacting, Christ-exalting
resources from his earliest days as an evangelist
and pastor until these days of his semi-retirement.

His life has been a profound gift of service to the
Church of God. He represents others like himself
who have committed to lives of integrity,
vision-casting and sacrifice.

For 15 years he and I worked as partnering pastors.
I never once saw him compromise his convictions
or fail to stay focused on the great
destiny of the church.

To me he has been the iron that sharpens iron
and the friend that sticks closer than a brother.

Discover More Online

Check out the additional materials and resources on the Web site that accompanies this book, *www.greatcommission.cc.*

Contents

Acknowledgements

A book is seldom the creation of one person, and this one is no exception.

First, let me express my profound appreciation to the members of the Executive Committee—Tim Hill, Mark Williams, David Griffis and Wallace Sibley. These men, seasoned veterans of the pastorate and administrative leadership, carry the burden of the church on a daily basis. They are convinced, as I am, that the church's effectiveness lies in our commitment to hear and obey Christ's commission for the church to be a soulwinning, disciple-making fellowship.

In putting together these chapters, I invited a team of competent churchmen—Floyd Carey, Bill George, Tony Lane, Mike Chapman, Leonard Albert and Tom George—to work with me. Out of the background of their experience, well over 200 years of practice when the years of their ministries are added together, they have thought through the implications of the themes of this book with me. Together we have sifted through principles, ideas, programs that have evidenced success in the past and in our contemporary setting, and we have written down the essence of what we have explored. Readers will benefit from the input of these church leaders, and I have enjoyed working with them.

The personnel of Pathway Press have been pleasant to work with, particularly Mike Burnett, director of Printing, who always works to ensure a quality product.

Virgie Parker, my executive assistant, is a multitalented individual with a delightful combination of intelligence, skills, grace and a strong work ethic. She has helped move the book along in the production schedule.

Peggy, my wife of 39 years and my partner in ministry, has endured hours of my talking through the concepts printed in these pages. She is an excellent counselor and a spirited advisor. She makes my life happier, and I love her.

—Raymond F. Culpepper, D.D.

Foreword

Oswald J. Smith, noted missionary pastor, declared, "The supreme task of the church is the evangelization of the world." He further emphasized this by stating, "If God wills the evangelization of the world, and you refuse to support missions, then you are opposed to the will of God."

Dr. Raymond F. Culpepper, general overseer of the Church of God, presented three emphases at the 72nd International General Assembly. One of those was the Great Commission. He underscored the importance of the missional mandate given to every church and every believer. This volume shares that burden.

In seven compelling chapters, Dr. Culpepper reminds us that "we live to finish the mission." We must do it, and we will. Jesus has given us the Holy Spirit as our dynamic enabler.

The Great Commission is a biblical mandate. This is highlighted in Chapter 1 and more fully developed in the following chapters of the commission's emphasis upon connecting, converting, discipling, equipping and empowering every believer.

Dr. Culpepper shares ten connecting points to assist disciples in revealing their God-given love for all people. God uses relationships to express this love; this becomes the open door for evangelism. His discussion of cultures and postmodern thought is most helpful in knowing how to deal with unbelievers. He gives special insights about how nonbelievers view Christians, and the power of personal testimony.

Evangelism is not complete without discipleship. Dr. Culpepper reminds us that the Great Commission is not just a call to go and evangelize, but also to make disciples. He draws from his wealth of experience as a pastor to give suggestions on the discipling of believers. "Discipleship," he says, "is not an instantaneous act." The target for discipleship must be "production of saints."

At the end of each chapter is a list of discussion points that aid in reviewing and sharing the information given. These can provide the basis for a lively forum for interaction with others.

This book provides a gold mine of ideas for fulfilling the Great Commission. The illustrations capture the imagination, and the practical ideas can be developed for any setting. It is compelling reading from a heart committed to fulfilling the charge of Christ.

Every member is a missionary. Absorbing and practicing the principles presented in this volume will help God's people fulfill that mission, "until all have heard."

—Douglas LeRoy
General Director
Church of God World Missions

Introduction

My son, Raymond, is quite a war history buff. When one of the businessmen in our church in Birmingham offered us free tickets to hear General Norman Schwarzkopf, the hero of the first Gulf War, speak at one of those high-dollar banquets, it was a no-brainer. What an evening!

We met the general, shook his hand and had a photograph with him. I keep the picture in my office as a reminder of two things: one, a cherished evening with my son, and two, a challenging question posed by the general.

In the course of his speech, he told of the tough task of keeping the allied coalition together. There were 29 nations in the coalition from all over the world—North America, Middle East, Asia, Australia, Europe and Central and South America. At times during the top-brass war room strategy sessions, he said opinions would differ, religions would clash, policies would divide and tempers would flare. At those volatile, mercurial moments, Schwarzkopf would stop the banter and ask one question: "Gentlemen, why are we here?"

The answer in chorus was always the same, "To kick Saddam Hussein out of Kuwait!" The meeting would settle down and go forward.

I ask the Church of God today: Why is the church here?

Think about it. Why did Jesus become flesh, live, die, rise and return to the Father? Why did the Holy Spirit come? Why is the church here? Why are you and I here?

It was finished, indeed, but He was not finished. The plan of salvation was finished, but the Savior had a church to build.

That dark Golgotha day when Jesus said, "It is finished," it was finished. He had said, "My food is to do the will of Him who sent Me, and to finish His work" (John 4:34). He had said, "For this purpose I came to this hour. . . . And I, if I am lifted up from the earth, will draw all peoples to Myself. This he said, signifying by what death He would die" (John 12:27, 32, 33). It was finished, indeed, but He was not finished. The plan of salvation was finished, but the Savior had a church to build. Between His resurrection and ascension He made clear what the church was to do. In fact, all four Gospels and the first chapter of Acts repeated His plan—even before the church was born at Pentecost.

It is called the Great Commission. *"The"* because there is one premier mission of the church. *"Great"* because the mission is preeminent. *"Commission"* because it is the assigned marching orders of the Spirit-filled church. Just as the Son finished the Father's work, the church—Christ's body—is divinely appointed to finish Christ's work.

Yes, it was finished; Jesus wasn't. Neither are we.

Why are we here? To partner with Christ by the Holy Spirit in carrying out the mission. He died for the mission. We live to finish the mission.

Although simple, His commission is challenging. Each of the five commission announcements emphasizes an underlying strategy.

Connecting

> *"Go into all the world and preach the gospel to every creature"* (Mark 16:15).

Go means to connect with the world around us. Connect with every culture, context, and color.

Converting

> *"Then He said to them, 'Thus it is written, and thus it was necessary for the Christ to suffer and to rise from the dead the third day, and that repentance and remission of sins should be preached in His name to all nations, beginning at Jerusalem'"* (Luke 24:46, 47).

Repentance and forgiveness of sins are exact words describing the conversion of a sinner. It's about rescuing the perishing, finding the lost, saving the sinner. The church can call it evangelism, soulwinning, fishing for men, but "unless one is born again, he cannot see the kingdom of God"

(John 3:3). "This is a faithful saying and worthy of all acceptance, that Christ Jesus came into the world to save sinners" (1 Timothy 1:15).

Discipling

> *"And Jesus came and spoke to them, saying, 'All authority has been given to Me in heaven and on earth. Go therefore and make disciples of all the nations, baptizing them in the name of the Father and of the Son and of the Holy Spirit, teaching them to observe all things that I have commanded you; and lo, I am with you always, even to the end of the age'"* (Matthew 28:18-20).

Just as newborn babies need more than a congratulatory pat on the back, so do new creations in Christ. The instant of their salvation they become disciples (learners, followers, students) who need discipling (teaching, leadership, instruction). Jesus knew the mortality rate would be high without discipling. That's why Paul said in 1 Timothy 2:2, "The things that you have heard from me among many witnesses, commit these to faithful men who will be able to teach others also."

Equipping

> *"So Jesus said to them again, 'Peace to you! As the Father has sent Me, I also send you"* (John 20:21).

Equipping is about furnishing all the resources needed to fulfill an assignment. The Father sent His Son fully furnished with anointing, power, and giftedness necessary to complete His work. Every believer not only has an assignment, but an anointing and gifting to serve effectively. It is the task of leaders in the church to help others discover their assignment. It is the task of each individual to develop and deploy his equipment.

Every believer not only has an assignment, but an anointing and gifting to serve effectively.

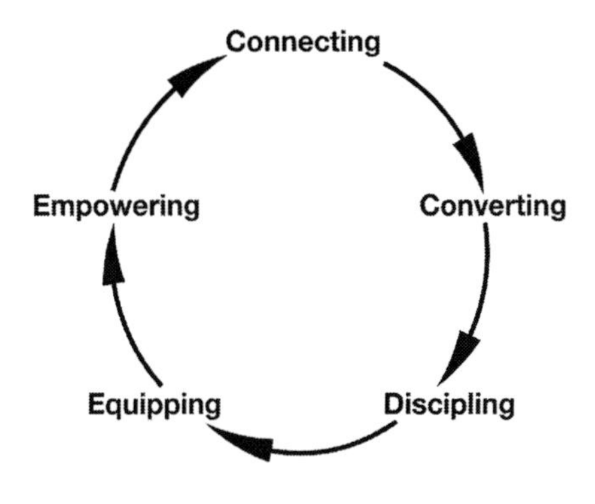

Empowering

"But you shall receive power when the Holy Spirit has come upon you and you shall be witnesses to Me in Jerusalem, and in all Judea and Samaria, and to the end of the earth" (Acts 1:8).

Empowering is twofold: it requires a knowledge of the task and the capacity to accomplish it. This Great Commission mission is gargantuan and overwhelmingly impossible without the power of the Holy Spirit. Believers accept the Spirit's power when they receive the baptism in the Holy Spirit. They actualize His power when they are set apart for a particular endeavor. The apostle Paul was empowered by the Holy Spirit in Acts 9:17; he was empowered again by the Holy Spirit when the leaders of the church in Antioch separated him for the specific work to which he had been called (see Acts 13:2).

The church is invited to process the Great Commission. Process? Yes. From the perspective of Jesus, this it what it looks like.

In my personal times of prayer and fasting, I have heard the still, quiet voice of the Holy Spirit calling me to the mission. As I travel around the world observing the work of the Holy Spirit, I'm reminded of the mission. When I'm in meeting with world denominational and parachurch leaders, I hear them speaking the same word of agreement with the Spirit.

The question has never been, will the church survive? Or will the church change? The question is, will the church embrace its mission with conviction?

The question has never been, will the church survive? Or will the church change? The question is, will the church embrace its mission with conviction? That is the supreme reason the church is here. We are on a mission. We are missionaries.

Readers of the Bible discover that God is a missionary.

In Genesis 3, He promises to send a Savior. In Genesis 12, He speaks to Abraham and sends him on a mission. In Exodus 19, He comes down to Egypt and delivers His people. In Isaiah 42:6, 7, He says, ""I, the Lord, have called you in righteousness; I will take hold of your hand. I will keep you and will make you to be a covenant for the people and a light for the Gentiles, to open eyes that are blind, to free captives from prison and to release from the dungeon those who sit in darkness." This is the work of a missionary.

Throughout the Word, God the Father manifests His coming and His sending to save a people for His glory. He chose a people for himself, then commissioned them to take His message to the nations. He visited Gentiles, such as Rahab and Ruth and Namaan. In the Psalms, He inspired more than 175 references that related to the nations of the earth coming to salvation in Him.

Jesus was a missionary. He knew why He came. In Matthew 20:28, He explained that He had not come to be served, but to serve and give His life a ransom for many. In John 10:11, He declared He would lay down His life for His sheep. In John 1, He revealed the mystery of His incarnation. In John 1:29, He is the lamb of God. In John 12, He showed the manner of His death; He will be lifted up and will draw all men to himself. He came to the earth and lived among men and became one with them that they could become one with Him. That is the work of a missionary.

I am convinced that God is calling His people to be a missionary people and His church a missionary church.

I am convinced that God is calling His people to be a missionary people and His church a missionary church. The church will fulfill its purpose by a great commitment to the Great Commission

Before the foundation of the world, God decided the death of His only Son would not be in vain. More people are now alive on Planet Earth than have lived in history, nearly seven billion. The greatest harvest of souls ever is going on. Around the world 3,000 souls are saved every 25 minutes.[1] The Great Commission is coming to your house. Embrace it. Practice it. Process it.

In recent months, I have read that the Church of God is recognized as the 25th largest denomination in the United States. Considering that 224 North American denominations exist, that's pretty good. Reports indicate that the only two evangelical churches experiencing growth last year were the Church of God (2.04 percent) and the Assemblies of God (.96 percent). [2]

Am I boasting? No. I'm saying we have a responsibiity to the 21st century to rise from our Pentecostal foundation and go forward to achieve our God-ordained destiny. We have come to the Kingdom for such a time as this. Pluralism, terrorism, recession, starvation, genocide, abuse, immorality, war, shattered lives, broken homes, disease, prejudice, sin, idolatry and materialism oppose the mission of God. The church must respond with Great Commission action. If not now, when? If not us, who?

I remember the words of John F. Kennedy when he accepted his party's nomination for the presidency. He said,

---

1 James Rutz, *Megashift* (Colorado Springs: Empowerment Press, 2005), 25. Rutz says that 175,000 Christians are added to the church daily, calculating conversion rates minus deaths.

2 Eileen W. Lindner, *2009 Yearbook of American & Canadian Churches* (Nashville: Abingdon Press, 2009), 11.

> *The New Frontier of which I speak is not a set of promises—it is a set of challenges. It sums up not what I intend to offer the American people, but what I intend to ask of them. . . . It holds out the promise of more sacrifice instead of more security.* [3]

I call the Church of God to the challenge of the Great Commission. I ask of the church not security, but sacrifice.

The Great Commission is the solution.

—Raymond Culpepper, D.D.

3 John F. Kennedy, *"Address of Senator John F. Kennedy Accepting the Democratic Party Nomination for the Presidency of the United States"* 15 July 1960, John F. Kennedy Presidential Library and Museum, Boston, Massachusetts.

Chapter 1

Theology—
The Foundation of the Commission

> *And Jesus came and spoke to them, saying, "All authority has been given to Me in heaven and on earth. Go therefore and make disciples of all the nations, baptizing them in the name of the Father and of the Son and of the Holy Spirit, teaching them to observe all things that I have commanded you; and lo, I am with you always, even to the end of the age"* (Matthew 28:18-20).

It has been called "the Magna Carta of the church," "the marching orders of the church" and "the last great mandate." It has formed the basis of slogans such as "The last command of Christ is the first priority of the church"; and "If the commission of an earthly king can be considered an honor, how can a commission from a heavenly king be considered a sacrifice?"; and"Any church that is not seriously involved in helping fulfill the Great Commission has forfeited its biblical right to exist."

Despite the importance of the Commission, it is amazing how few people know much about it.

Despite the importance of the Commission, however, it is amazing how few people know much about it. A survey conducted a few years ago by a major research group reveals widespread ignorance of common Christian terms. Researchers asked a sample group of 1,210 adults to define Great Commission, evangelical, John 3:16, and gospel. In each case, only a small minority gave accurate answers. Even "born-again Christians" had trouble answering.

Only nine percent of the respondents accurately defined Great Commission. About 75 percent of born-again Christians could not offer a definition.

Clear but Disregarded

With a message given so clearly, how can it be misunder-stood, ignored, disobeyed, or otherwise disregarded? Nevertheless, the Great Commission has not always found its rightful place in the heart of the church.

Some have insisted that this instruction was meant only for the apostles and for first-century believers. This can be easily refuted from the text itself. In the same breath in which Jesus gave directions to His followers about their mission, He also said, "I'll be with you always, to the end of the age." Obviously more than the disciples were in view in this assurance from the Master. The apostles would die within a generation; however, the promise is "to the end of the age." Jesus clearly had the whole church through the ages in view when He gave both the Commission and the assurance of His presence. He knew His disciples faced tremendous difficulties and would need this assurance of His presence and power.

The situation is not much changed in the 21st century. The inability to defend the faith, the threat of hostile religions, the uncertainty of political conditions, the difficulty that accompanies a personal change of venue, the complications of economic realities—all these and more are enough to tempt a stalwart soul to fear and doubt.

A Question of Authority

It was for this reason, no doubt, that Jesus prefaced His Commission to His followers with the assurance of His power.

The disciples can anticipate victory in carrying out Christ's commission because His authority extends beyond the realm of the physical and political to the spiritual.

When Jesus said, "All authority is given to me," he uses the exacting word, *exousia. Exousia* carries with it the idea of active power, divine, irresistible influence; the complete ability to do what He desires. If the word itself is not still insufficient to banish doubt and fear, Christ adds that the extent of His power is "in heaven and in earth."

The disciples can anticipate victory in carrying out Christ's commission because His authority extends beyond the realm of the physical and political to the spiritual. He possesses authority over this world and all its dimensions. His power rules over demons and devils and rulers of darkness and all spiritual powers.

Believers can witness to the next door neighbor because Jesus' power extends to the house next door. They can testify to the clerk at the store because His power is there, too. They can help start the new church in the next town because Jesus is all-powerful in that town, too. They can get on a plane and fly to a foreign country because Jesus' power is not limited by national boundaries. A commission is only as good as the authority that backs it up. The Great Commission advances with full authority from the King of kings and the Lord of lords.

He can exercise His will wherever we carry His Word, because He has all power in heaven and on earth. Until the time of this Great Commission proclamation, that power had been limited. When Jesus came to earth, He laid aside the independent self-exercise of the divine attributes. In glory His power had been limitless, just as His Father's was limitless. During His earthly ministry in a human form, His omnipresence and omnipotence seems to have been diminished.

But now there are no limitations. All authority!

Servant of God, do not doubt. Do not hesitate. Do not fall back. Do not lose heart. You are serving the One who has all power!

We began the church in Birmingham in 1980, with no building, no property and no money, and were anxious to get moving. I knew about a wealthy business owner, CEO of a Fortune 500 company headquartered in the city, John Harbert III, of Harbert Construction Company. The company had major construction projects around the world. His office was only 10 minutes from where I lived, so I decided to see him and present my vision for the church and invite him to buy into it. I thought to ask him for a financial gift that would put the church on its feet.

The morning of my proposed visit, I got ready to go and was rehearsing my presentation. Faced with the prospect of entering the office of a multimillionaire, I confess I was intimated and fearful. Evidently Peggy, my wife, saw those feelings reflected in my countenance.

"Come back here," she admonished me, "You can't go looking like that. Stand up straight. Hold up your head. You are a called, anointed preacher of the gospel. Your God owns the cattle on a thousand hills. You are a representative of the King of kings. Don't make him or me ashamed!" She told me what I needed to hear.

To make a long story short, I went to the office, but I didn't see Mr. Harbert. In my nauïveté, I entered the building without an appointment, not even thinking about needing one. After searching through the large headquarters building, I finally located a secretary of a secretary, who told me that the CEO was visiting a project in South America. I was never able to contact him about a gift to the church. The visit was almost a waste of time; however, out of it I learned a vital lesson (prompted by Peggy): If any one of us is on a mission for the Kingdom, we are under the authority of the King. We must function in His full authority!

The Scope of the Commission

When Christ told the church what He wanted accomplished, He chose His words carefully. He let them know that it was His will that they go—wherever their journeys would take them—and make disciples among all the groups of people they came into contact with. Making disciples begins with the proclamation of the saving word, but it is not complete until believers have been baptized and taught.

"Going" undergirds the Great Commission. The church has chosen to emphasize different aspects of going at different times and according to who is pronouncing the emphasis. Local church pastors concentrate on near neighbors, the people down the street or even the relatives and friends of the church members. Evangelism people talk about home missions, or going to those in nearby areas or other states in the same country. World Missions people highlight the "uttermost," people in other lands, in recent years concentrating on Unreached Peoples, those large populations among whom no churches or few churches presently exist.

Who is to be made disciples? According to the Word, it is** panta ta ethne* . . . ***"all the peoples."

We must not become distracted debating which of these target groups we should go to. All of them are in focus in Christ's words.

Disciple Who?

Who is to be made disciples? According to the Word, it is *panta ta ethne* . . . "all the peoples." The familiar translation, "all the *nations*," can cause a bit of a misunderstanding at this point. We know what a nation is: it is a political division with its borders and its government.

Ethne is something different. *Ethne* means something like what we mean when we say "ethnics." It is a group of people who believe they have something in common with each other, usually things like language, culture and heritage. One nation may embrace many *ethne,* and usually does. The United States is a nation, but it is made up of a tapestry of Whites, Blacks, Hispanics, Europeans, Asians and—in fact—many subdivisions among these groups. Jesus wants disciples made among all the different groups.

A beautiful scene is envisioned in heaven, according to Revelation 7:9, which declares:

> *After these things I looked, and behold, a great multitude which no one could number, of all nations, tribes, peoples and tongues, standing before the throne and before the Lamb, clothed with white robes, with palm branches in their hands.*

Luke 15 affirms that there is joy and rejoicing in heaven over one sinner who repents. I can imagine the special sense of celebration that must be felt in heaven when a new voice is heard, a voice from a people group never before reached with the gospel. It is the first day since the beginning of time that a voice from that tribe or tongue has ever cried out to God! What a celebration!

The emphasis of the Commission is upon connecting, converting, discipling, equipping and empowering everyone. The vision is of winning one, two, five, ten, a hundred. When the Christian community is strong enough, it will influence society and eventually society can be transformed. The kingship and lordship of Christ can be acknowledged throughout the whole people group. That is His goal and plan.

When the Christian community is strong enough, it will influence society and eventually society can be transformed.

The Great Commission is for every member of the church. It is for the one who witnesses to near neighbors, the one who plants churches and the one who goes to lands far away.

The late Sam Shoemaker, an Episcopalian bishop, summed up the situation this way: "In the Great Commission the Lord has called us to be—like Peter—fishers of men. We've turned the commission around so that we have become merely keepers of the aquarium. Occasionally I take some fish out of your fish bowl and put them into mine, and you do the same with my bowl. But we're all tending the same fish."[1]

1 Quoted by Em Griffin in *The Mindchangers* (Wheaton, Illinois: Tyndale House, 1976), 151.

The Commission in Action

Jesus said, "I will build my church (Matthew 16:18). Paul, reflecting on the development of a local church in Corinth, wrote: "I planted, Apollos watered, but God gave the increase … for we are God's fellow workers" (1 Corinthians 3:6, 9).

The Book of Acts witnesses the Great Commission in action. It is the church that sends missionaries, witnesses and church planters. Converts are won and discipling takes place.

The Book of Acts witnesses the Great Commission in action. It is the church that sends missionaries, witnesses and church planters. Converts are won and discipling takes place.

The establishment and growth of a church is the product of God's working by His Spirit through His servants. It is clearly the church as an instrument and an end that Christ had in mind when He gave the commission to His people.

It is against the background of successful obedience to the Great Commission and its resulting establishment of new congregations that the astounding claim of C. Peter Wagner can be understood: "The single most effective evangelistic methodology under heaven is planting new churches."[2]

---

2 C. Peter Wagner, *Church Planting for a Greater Harvest* (Ventura, Calif., Regal, 1990), 7.

A Theological Framework

Biblical and theological reflection teach Christians that hearing and obeying Christ's Great Commission must be rooted in an understanding of the character and purposes of God, the reality of the Incarnation, the dynamic of the kingdom of God and the example of the New Testament.

Missio Dei (God's Mission)

The beginning point for developing a theological undergirding for Great Commission obedience is the missiological concept of *missio dei* (God's mission). This is the strong conviction that what Christians do in contributing to the expansion of God's kingdom is not the invention or program of human beings, but flows from the character and purposes of God.

Those who obey the Great Commission do not go nor are sent only because of their own initiative, but because God, the original Sender, puts it in their hearts to obey. God's sending initiative is richly traced in the Bible. It begins with the *protoevangelium* of Genesis 3:15, where it immediately becomes clear that grace is not an afterthought, but it enters the world side by side with sin. Although the serpent has caused the Fall, the seed of woman (Christ) would bruise his head. Here at the beginning of mankind's history it is indicated that God would send One who, as it is revealed later in the Scriptures, would redeem fallen men and women.

Those who obey the Great Commission do not go nor are sent only because of their own initiative, but because God, the original Sender, puts it in their hearts to obey.

The *missio dei* comes into clearer focus in the experience of Abraham, where the Sending God calls a man to leave his homeland and go to an unknown destination. God's plan, according to the directions He gave, was that "In you all the families of the earth shall be blessed" (Genesis 12:3). History reveals that this blessing would come ultimately through Jesus Christ, the descendent of Abraham.

In the Book of Isaiah, the first five chapters paint a dark picture of a despairing world and disclose a disappointed God. In chapter 6, however, He shows His care and concern by calling a prophet who would voice judgment and invite the people to return to God. The oft-quoted encounter of God with the prophet declares, "Also I heard the voice of the Lord say: 'Whom shall I send, and who will go for Us?' Then I said, 'Here am I. Send me'" (Isaiah 6:8). The Sending God seeks one who will deliver His message of judgment and redemption.

The universal character of the *missio dei* is revealed in Jonah. God cares not only for His own people, but also He is concerned about the whole world. He sends a reluctant prophet to take a message of judgment and a call for repentance to one of the most powerful and wicked cities of that ancient day. In response to their repentance, God pardons them.

God's sending character is divulged clearly in 2 Corinthians 5:20, "Now then, we are ambassadors for Christ, as though God were pleading through us: we implore you in Christ's behalf, be reconciled to God." An ambassador is one sent from the seat of government to another nation to represent his ruler. God sends men today to represent Him. All of our going is a reflection of His sending character. All witnesses or preachers who ever undertake the daunting task of establishing a new outpost of God's kingdom should rest in the assurance that they have been commissioned to do so by the King.

The Incarnation

The Incarnation provides both a model and a motivation for those who fulfill the Great Commission. It is a *model* in that Jesus Christ reveals what God is like, and His obedient followers have the same challenge. The people to whom they tell the story of God's love will need to see through their lives something of the likeness of Christ. It is a *motivation* because Jesus taught, "As the Father has sent Me, I also send you" (John 20:21).

The Incarnation provides both a model and a motivation for those who fulfill the Great Commission.

"And the Word became flesh and dwelt among us, and we beheld His glory," declares John 1:14. The mystery of the Incarnation can never be fully comprehended by humans, but it conveys God's love for men and women in a way that nothing else could have done. Paul further elaborates, "For you know the grace of our Lord Jesus Christ, that though He was rich, yet for your sakes He became poor, that you through His poverty might become rich" (2 Corinthians 8:9).

Although God in His dealings with humans has manifested Himself in diverse manners, the writer of Hebrews explains: "God, who at various times and in various ways spoke in time past to the fathers by the prophets, has in these last days spoken to us by His Son (1:1, 2). The uniqueness of the Incarnation took the world by surprise and masked His true identity except to those to whom He revealed himself. The incarnational motivation for those who take the Great Commission seriously comes directly from the lips of Jesus himself, who said plainly, "As the Father has sent Me, I also send you" (John 20:21).

How did God send Jesus? He commissioned Him to a distinct culture in a defined location at a certain time for a precise purpose. He was a male Jew who lived in first-century Palestine, spoke Aramaic, and had a given mission that He himself explained:

> *The Spirit of the Lord is upon Me, because He has anointed Me to preach the gospel to the poor; He has sent Me to heal the brokenhearted, to proclaim liberty to the captives and recovery of sight to the blind, to set at liberty those who are oppressed; to proclaim the acceptable year of the Lord* (Luke 4:18).

After His earthly followers had witnessed His fulfillment of the mission, He instructed them, "I am sending you to do what the Father sent me to do."

The Incarnation is an "enfleshment," and that has implications for all who would let the Great Commission guide their lives. Missionaries are sent not only to proclaim, but also to "enflesh" ministry, that is, to live it out. Those who obey Christ's commission look for ways to identify with those among whom they work, ways to enter into their lives, care for them, help them, show compassion to them, lift them up. That is the way Jesus ministered; and He is the example. "If presence without proclamation is unintelligible, proclamation without presence is unconvincing," is the way church planter Stuart Murray put it in *Church Planting: Laying Foundations.*[3]

The Incarnation also teaches Christ-followers to be culturally sensitive, seeking for contextually appropriate ways to share the gospel and build up the church. Clearly this calls for a balanced approach to ministry. Christ-followers must not allow culture to shape the church apart from an awareness of what the church ought biblically to be. On the other hand, the church that is planted or nurtured should not be foreign to its community. Paul wrote, "I have become all things to all men, that I might by all means save some" (1 Corinthians 9:22).

On a practical level, for purposes of illustration, Bill George told me of a visit to a small town in the jungles of Honduras, where the houses along the street were built of adobe and wood. In the middle of town he happened upon an American Southern-style concrete block, stuccoed church building with Georgian columns supporting a front porch, totally out of context with the community. Whatever else the church building communicated to passers-by, it proclaimed, "I'm foreign; I don't really belong here!" Incarnation demands that missionaries, church planters and witnesses

3 Stuart Murray, *Church Planting: Laying Foundations* (Scottdale, Penn.: Herald Press, 2001), 112.

(you and I) will assume the fabric of the community where we minister, to the extent possible, and not attempt to import our own culture. Culture is not sin. All people have their distinct culture. It is simply the knowledge, values, attitudes, and behavior characteristic of a particular social group. But good missionaries understand that if they operate out of their home culture rather than that of the people to whom they ministry, they will limit their effectiveness. I can't help but wonder how many Hondurans would be attracted by the foreign-style architecture of the church building.

The Kingdom of God

Those who seriously carry out the Great Commission need to understand that the church and the kingdom of God are not the same. While the church is a community, the kingdom is an activity: God extending His reign throughout Creation. The two are closely related, but they are not precisely the same. The central message of Jesus is the kingdom of God (see Matthew 13), while the church is mentioned by Him only peripherally. The Kingdom is dynamic and the church can be static. Those who observe with spiritual eyes know that God is at work outside the church as well as within and through it. The Gospels represent the Kingdom as a spiritual commonwealth embracing all those adopting God's principles and motives in life and meeting the moral and spiritual requirements He lays down, while, on the other hand, the church is a society based upon the principles of the Kingdom in which the members are held together by outward ties of fellowship.

Those who observe with spiritual eyes know that God is at work outside the church as well as within and through it.

> *If they are functioning properly, churches will be agents of the kingdom, signposts to the kingdom, sacraments of the kingdom, provisional representations of the kingdom proclaiming and demonstrating the kingdom, pointing to what is coming when the kingdom is established, but they cannot be equated with the kingdom.*[4]

The Kingdom is a kingdom of power. The signs of the Kingdom include signs and wonders. In this light, the Great Commission becomes spiritual warfare, a way of advancing the kingdom, because it is a commitment to establish a cell of resistance (the church) in a world hostile to God. With a Kingdom mentality in place, Christ-followers understand that witnessing or planting a church is not an ultimate goal. The ultimate goal is the expansion of the Kingdom. Living under the rule of God is not a solitary calling, but an invitation to join a movement cooperating with God in the advancement of His Kingdom. The Kingdom is the overarching reality; the church is an expression of the Kingdom. The Kingdom is the reign of God in the lives of His people. Calling people to that relationship is a function of the church. Those who incarnate the Great Commission rejoice in praying, "Your kingdom come, Your will be done on earth as it is in heaven."

---

4 Stuart Murray, *Church Planting: Laying Foundations* (Scottdale, Penn.: Herald Press, 2001), 47.

The Formation of New Testament Churches

When Jesus proclaimed that He would build His church, He announced His resolve for the people of God to gather in community. The New Testament vision is for explicit and intentional commitment to Jesus to be expressed in mutual worship, edification, caring and fellowship. The gospel knows nothing of Lone Ranger Christianity; believers were together and had all things in common.

> *Jesus seems to have perceived his disciples as becoming an identifiable, visible community of witnesses within the larger society . . . These local churches became the sustaining energizers for evangelism, cultural or political reform, reconciliation, justice and service in the community.*[5]

The Great Commandment

The preamble to the Great Commission is the Great Commandment. When Jesus was asked which commandment was greatest, He answered, "You shall love the Lord your God with all your heart, and with all your soul, and with all your mind. This is the great and foremost commandment. The second is like it, You shall love your neighbor as yourself" (Matthew 22:37-39). In the words of David Ferguson, "The Great Commission capsulizes what we *do,* while the Great Commandment embodies who we *are.*"[6]

---

5 David W. Shenk and Ervin Stutzman, *Creating Communities of the Kingdom* (Scottdale, Penn.: Herald Press, 1988), 92.

6 David Ferguson, *The Great Commandment Principle* (Wheaton, Il.: Tyndale Publishing, 1998) 37.

"The Great Commission capsulizes what we do, while the Great Commandment embodies who we are."

If the Great Commandment is not working in believers' lives, the Great Commission will not work in the church.

The church, which—by the way—is a people, not a building, is the aroma of God's love to the world. When we love God supremely, we are empowered to give without giving out, to give without an expectation of return. A church that tries to connect without first loving God totally will eventually become fatigued and run out of energy. Moreover, a church that tries to connect with lost people without love will begin to view those people as unreachable. A great commitment to the Great Commandment and the Great Commission is the Church of God's greatest challenge. The God-kind of love—*agape*—means the church cannot love lost people any more and it cannot love them any less.

Going with the gospel will be most effective when we go with love and compassion in our hearts. The tragic Indian Ocean tsunami of December 2004 that took the lives of 225,000 in 11 countries opened a wide door for the Church of God to reach out to hurting people in several countries. Relief efforts were particularly effective in Indonesia.

Going with the gospel will be most effective when we go with love and compassion in our hearts.

The Aceh province of Sumatra, where the most damage was recorded, has traditionally been a stronghold of militant Islam and hostility to Westerners. As a result of the loving outreach following the earthquake and tidal wave, however, the people in this area have now embraced a more welcoming attitude toward the message of Christianity.

Paul expressed it best, as the Holy Spirit revealed it to him, in 1 Corinthians 13:4-8.

> *Love suffers long and is kind; love does not envy; love does not parade itself, is not puffed up; does not behave rudely, does not seek its own, is not provoked, thinks no evil; does not rejoice in iniquity, but rejoices in the truth; bears all things, believes all things, hopes all things, endures all things. Love never fails.*

As is apparent in this exhortation, love is a decision and action, not just an emotion.

Love is the essence of God. God loved; He gave. God is love. When one sees Christ on the cross, he is looking at God's portrait of love. A man asked, "Jesus, how much do you love me?" Jesus opened His arms wide, then He died.

Theological Points

1. Identify the locations in the four Gospels and the Book of Acts of Christ's pronouncement called "The Great Commission."
2. What is the significance of the Bible's use of the word *exousia* for "power"?
3. At what point can a believer be considered, legitimately, a disciple?
4. When Christ gave His commission to make disciples "of all nations," what is the true meaning of His instruction?
5. State in one sentence the meaning of the term "*missio dei.*"
6. How did God send Jesus? State the specific mission Christ was given. In what way is it similar to the kind of mission God gives to individuals today?
7. The chapter tells of the architectural design of a particular church in Honduras. What is the significance of that story for an understanding of the Incarnation?
8. Are the church and the Kingdom the same thing? Why or why not?
9. When the 2004 Indian Ocean tsunami struck the province of Aceh on the island of Sumatra in Indonesia, what was the effect that resulted for the church?
10. Explore the implication of this sentence: "A great commitment to the Great Commandment and the Great Commission is the Church of God's greatest challenge."

Chapter 2

Connecting—The Key to the Commission

And Jesus came and spoke to them, saying, "All authority has been given to Me in heaven and on earth. Go therefore and make disciples of all the nations, baptizing them in the name of the Father and of the Son and of the Holy Spirit, teaching them to observe all things that I have commanded you; and lo, I am with you always, even to the end of the age (Matthew 28:18-20).

It looked as if my dad was going to follow in his father's footsteps—alcoholism. The first three years Dad and Mother were married, life was a struggle. Dad began drinking more and more. Mother prayed continually.

One night as she was praying, the Holy Spirit led her to 1 Corinthians 13. As she read the verses, suddenly the first part of verse eight seemed to leap off the page and take root in her heart: Love never fails.

She knew God had given her the promise that if she would love Dad, he would be saved. She clung to the assurance and persevered in prayer. In the months that followed, Dad's drinking worsened; still, she prayed and held to the promise, never mentioning to anyone about 1 Corinthians 13:8.

One Sunday afternoon, after a drinking binge, Dad was miraculously saved and delivered. Two weeks later he was baptized in the Holy Spirit. One week after that, he was asked to preach his first sermon. Talk about a miracle!

Dad went to the church that night without a prepared sermon. He knew nothing about the Bible, sermon preparation, or preaching. He had nothing, and he was in a panic. While the service was underway, he slipped out of his seat and went down into the basement of the little building to ask the Lord to give him something to say.

The reason love does not fail is because God is love and God cannot fail.

"O God," he wept and pleaded, "If you will help me this once, I'll never doubt your calling on my life to preach!"

Wiping the tears from his eyes, and trembling with fear, he held the Bible in his hands and let it fall open. A single sentence was illuminated by the Holy Spirit and that sentence became the text of his sermon: 1 Corinthians 13:8, "Love never fails."

Dad did not know until later that his first sermon was the fulfillment of God's love promise to my mother.

The reason love does not fail is because God is love and God cannot fail. God is the essence, existence, and expression of love. Love is *not* God; God is love. True *agape* love is not an emotion. Love is about will, decision, and action. God wills to love, decides with love, acts in love. Love is giving without giving out. The Great Commission turns on love.

It Begins With Going

When Jesus said, "Go into all the world," He was not just telling Christians to travel. He was instructing them to connect, relate, establish rapport with the people in the world. As the Father loved the world and sent His Son to redeem the world, Jesus sends all Christians with the commission to love their neighbors (see John 3:16; Galatians 4:4, 5).

I walked down a street in the inner city of Athens, Greece, with Pastor Anastasios Aronis. I saw a man passed out in a doorway, another rummaging through a garbage dumpster, and others trying to find drugs for their addiction, while a prostitute stood nearby on a street corner.

"Some people think we should move from this location to a better part of the city," the pastor explained, "but we believe God placed us here to minister to these people." I observed as he smiled, greeted, and touched people. That's love.

I visited an orphanage in Jakarta, Indonesia, located at the city dump where literally thousands of people live off the trash of the city. Their dwellings are made from discarded tin, cardboard, and broken bricks and stones. Their furniture is culled from the hundreds of acres of garbage.

I was introduced to three children who had arrived at the orphanage the night before, the youngest hot with typhoid fever. Veronica Backer is a registered nurse who directs the children's home. Poppi Smith, wife of Tommy Smith, a Church of God missionary, feeds several hundred children there each week. Why? Love.

I had breakfast just yesterday with a pastor who is a seminary graduate and Bible scholar par excellence. He is an extraordinary leader with keen people skills. "I believe I could build and lead a large congregation as a pastor," he said, "but that is not my calling. I am called to the professional marketplace to those who have no church or spiritual direction. I don't have to compete or be like anyone else. This is my assignment." Hearing his testimony, I say, "That is love!"

The shortest distance between the lost and the saved is the straight line of love.

When Paul said, "The love of Christ compels us," he meant either Christ's love for him, or his love for Christ, or the love of Christ in him for the world. I choose to think he meant all three!

The Pharisees, to whom Jesus spoke the Great Commandment, never got it. People are not drawn to superior doctrine, impressive reasoning, or holy hierarchy. The whole love thing went right over their heads, missing their hearts completely. The shortest distance between the lost and the saved is the straight line of love.

Eugene Peterson sums it up in 1 Corinthians 13:1-8 in *The Message*.

> If I speak with human eloquence and angelic ecstasy but don't love, I'm nothing but the creaking of a rusty gate. If I speak God's Word with power, revealing all his mysteries and making everything plain as day, and if I have faith that says to a mountain, "Jump," and it jumps, but I don't love, I'm nothing. If I give everything I own to the poor and even go to the stake to be burned as a martyr, but I don't love, I've gotten nowhere. So, no matter what I say, what I believe, and what I do, I'm bankrupt without love.
>
> Love never gives up.
> Love cares more for others than for self.
> Love doesn't want what it doesn't have.
> Love doesn't strut,
> Doesn't have a swelled head,
> Doesn't force itself on others,
> Isn't always "me first,"
> Doesn't fly off the handle,
> Doesn't keep score of the sins of others,
> Doesn't revel when others grovel,
> Takes pleasure in the flowering of truth,
> Puts up with anything,
> Trusts God always,
> Always looks for the best,
> Never looks back,
> But keeps going to the end.
>
> Love never dies.

Going into all the world requires connecting. Connecting is loving. But how can it be made practical? What does the love connection have to do with a missionary assignment?

Ten Connecting Points

1. Pray. Christians can do something after they pray, but they have done nothing until they pray. Prayer enriches love for God and others.

Family prayer—Write down a prayer unique to each member of the family and make that prayer part of daily intercessions.

Prayer walking—Pray on daily walks through the neighborhood for the people who live nearby.

Prayer driving—Driving to and from work, switch the radio off and pray for the people in the churches, schools, businesses and parks. Doug Small tells about a church in Missouri whose people dedicated a period of days to driving through their city, praying for the people whose homes they passed. The pastor usually participated, but one Friday night he was unable to go along. The men grouped themselves several to a car and drove along, praying. In one of the cars a man recognized a house they had passed and told the others he knew the man who lived there, and that he was unconverted. The driver backed up the car and, without making their presence known, they prayed for the friend's conversion. Late that night, the pastor received a call from a man who said, "I've got to talk to a preacher. You don't know me, but I have a friend who goes to your church. I need God. Will you come and pray with me?"

The pastor went and prayed for the man, and he was saved. The next morning when he met with the praying men to discuss their experiences that week, he told them about the late night call and the man who had been converted.

"It has to be a miracle," one of the men responded. "That's the very house where we prayed last night!"

2. **Learn more about culture**. Culture is the window through which people view, interact, and interpret the environment. It is the personal and social perspective of the values, attitudes, behavior and morals that have been integrated into a people's definition of the world. It is the way a person develops the art of interfacing with society. Culture determines the way life, words, actions, and attitudes are interpreted.

The Church of God of the early- to mid-20th century basically had to relate to one culture: post-war, conservative, agrarian, Southeastern, monolingual. Beginning in the 1970s and '80s, a shift began taking place. Fair trade agreements, a prospering economy, a pervasive Internet and mass people-group migrations shrunk the globe. Added to all of this was the transformation of the generations that changed the cultures inside homes. Each generation developed its own culture. Local has become global. Leonard Sweet calls it, "Glocal."[1]

The Church of God today in North America is a tapestry of multigenerational, multiethnic, multilinguistic, multicultural, multisocial people. The church is but a small picture of the larger world. The question now becomes, how can

1 Leonard Sweet, *Soul Tsunami* (Grand Rapids: Zondervan, 2001), 107. Sweet combines the word *local* with the word *global* to show that the worldview has changed from a neighborhood orientation to an international outlook.

Church of God missionaries interface with the world in the community? The answer is: The same way missionary Paul did.

The ends of the earth have come to the end of the street.

- *Go.* Paul had to travel great distances to reach other cultures. Today, Christians can go across town, or maybe next door. The ends of the earth have come to the end of the street.
- *Dialogue.* Where there are language barriers, interpreters can help to inquire about their culture, needs, hopes, and hurts.
- *Respect.* Difference in culture does not mean inferior—just different. People discern whether others are condescending or caring.
- *Provide opportunities.* Invite different cultures to interact with the church community. Many cultures have communities of believers who are looking for fellowship and facilities.
- *Anticipate adjustments.* There may be prejudices to overcome and issues to be resolved, but don't throw out the mission with the mess.
- *Don't cram.* Some people groups don't want to worship multiculturally. They prefer their own style of worship, leadership, and environment. Network with other churches and ministries who share the mission.
- *Keep Jesus central.* (Enough said.)

3. Understand Generational Ministry. Sociologists have identified generational groups and have taught about how to relate to them. The following chart, on the next page, compiled from various sources, tells about these groups.

Generational Characteristics

Categories	Builders/Veterans Traditionalists	Baby Boomers	Generation X	Generation Y Nexters
Birth Date	1925-1945	1946-1960	1961-1980	1981-2001
Population	55 million	76 million	60 million	74 million
Defining Events	WW I and WW II Great Depression Atomic Bomb	Cold War Civil Rights Vietnam Television	Roe vs. Wade Fall of Berlin Wall AIDS Computers	Terrorist attacks Internet Desert Storm Technology
View of family	Close family Married once	Dispersed family Divorce/remarriage	Latch-key kids Single parent/blended families	Loose family structure Single parent
View of authority	Honor and respect for leaders	Challenge leaders Never trust anyone over 30	Ignore leaders and don't try to become one	Respects authority but not awed by it
View of Technology	Hope to outlive it	Master it	Enjoy it	Employ it
Slogans	No Sweat	No Problem	No Fear	No Whatever Want it right now
Religious Characteristics	Committed to church Enjoy Bible study Loyal to denominations Worship in reverence	Committed to relationships Want to belong Want experiences with faith	Committed to family Short attention span Denominations not important Want less structure	Committed to family Biblically illiterate Spiritually hungry Multiple expressions of worship Highly tolerant and open
Characteristics	Hard workers Savers Patriotic Loyal to institutions Private Dependable	Educated Desire quality Cause-oriented	Neglected by parents Loyal to relationships Stressed out Self-reliant Skeptical Highly spiritual Survivors	Cherished by parents Groomed to achieve and excel Entrepreneurial hard workers who thrive on flexibility Most socially conscious Volunteerism high

4. **Become known as a caring church**. People all around the church are hurting. Some have suffered job loss and need help until they find employment. Couples are experiencing marital stress and need someone to offer counsel. Families need tutors for their children who are having difficulty with school. The list of needs in any community is lengthy. Fulfilling the Church Growth axiom, "Find a need and fill it," will allow the community to identify the church as a caring place.

5. **Cultivate relationships with lost people**. Research indicates the average believer has at least 20 relationships with unchurched people.[2] The immediate mission field for a church of 50 people is 1,000 individuals. What would happen if believers intentionally cultivated, developed, deepened those relationships? Investing time to listen, serve, pray for, and fellowship with others will bring a harvest. It might take months or years—but, there will be a harvest. Jesus told his disciples the harvest is plentiful, the laborers few (see Matthew 9:37).

Learn how lost people think. Most nonbelievers assume that church is for religious people, not real people. Most lost people are confused about basic truths.

- They think pluralistically. They believe there are many ways to God.
- They value tolerance. Their philosophy is "To each his own."

---

[2] Herb Miller, *How To Build a Magnetic Church* (Nashville: Abingdon Press, 1987), 33.

- They are pragmatists. For them the question is not, "Is it right or wrong," the question is, "Does it work?"
- They need love. The kind of love they need is not preachy or judgmental. (Missionaries don't convict of sin, the Holy Spirit is in charge of that).

6. **Do something significant for the community.** Whether individual or churchwide, the community always has physical needs: free use of a church facility, furnishing playground equipment for a city park, chaplaincy, building a house for a needy family. Missionaries do more serving outside the missionary outpost than inside. (Maybe that's why they call it an outpost.)

Missionaries do more serving outside the missionary outpost than inside.

---

7. **Learn from other missionaries and missional churches**. No one has to reinvent the wheel. There are many missional people and missional ministries around. Learning from them does not require the compromise of distinctives or convictions. Learning from effective people sharpens the tools to bring in the harvest.

8. **Discern the difference between preferences and essentials**. Because of my cultural and developmental experiences, I prefer a particular type of music, a certain mode of preaching, and a specific style of worship. I am reminded, however, that my missionary handbook teaches me to become "all things to all men, that I might by all means save some" (1 Corinthians 9:22). At the same time, I must "contend

earnestly for the faith which was once for all delivered to the saints" (Jude 3).

I recently attended the convention of the North America Church of God India Fellowship in Philadelphia with a large number of Malayalam-speakers in attendance. I did not understand much that was going on. The singing was characterized by an Indian tonal approach, markedly different from the songs I am accustomed to sing. When it came time to preach, I used my usual conversational, somewhat laid-back style of delivery. The interpreter, however, was accustomed to a rapid-fire, staccato way of preaching, and that's the way he preached my sermon. It was quite different, but the fact is—during that service I sincerely felt the presence of God!

It must break the heart of the Savior when the church builds walls of preference alienating the lost from the Cross. His death destroyed the wall of partition (see Matthew 27:51 and Ephesians 2:14, KJV). May the church not be guilty of building a wall of preference!

A pastor told me that the elders in his church came to him asking, "What can we do to stop our children from leaving the church?" He answered, "That depends on how much you are willing to change in order to keep them." They replied, "You lead us and we will follow you." Within a year the church grew by 300 new attenders. Their children stopped their exodus.

9. Be a missional church. "Missional is a way of thinking that challenges the church to re-form and reforge its understanding (theologically, spiritually and socially) so that it can relearn how to live and proclaim the gospel to the world."[3] The best way for a church to think of this is to consider its assignment from Christ to be a missionary church. A missionary sees circumstances as opportunities. A missionary is aware that commitment is contagious.

"Missional is a way of thinking that challenges the church to re-form and reforge its understanding (theologically, spiritually and socially) so that it can relearn how to live and proclaim the gospel to the world."

True missionaries are not concerned with credit, recognition, or appreciation, but should ask God to permit them to see at least one missionary opportunity every day. They will reap a harvest. They will start a movement. They will influence others. They will hear Christ say, "Well done!"

10. Remember the broken and backslidden. They come from a background of Christian families and churches and they populate every community. Many have been hurt by other church people, and some have self-inflicted wounds. Some have failed miserably. Some are hiding from their shame. They are road kill in a fast-driving world that seldom looks back. They don't need the church to connect, but to reconnect. Their Christian neighbors know most of them and their stories. They are prodigals, lost coins, scattered sheep, marred vessels.They

---

[3] Will Mancini, *Church Unique* (San Francisco: Jossey-Bass, 2008), 33.

need a missionary who will step just outside the door and lovingly give them an entrance with acceptance and hope.

I had breakfast with one of them today. What was a simple breakfast appointment to me meant the world to him. Remember the broken and backslidden.

I am moved by the apologia of the late Samuel Shoemaker, a New York clergyman. His heartfelt expression reveals a Christian's passion.

I Stand by the Door: An Apology for My Life

I stand by the door. I neither go too far in, nor stay too far out.
The door is the most important door in the world.
It is the door through which people walk when they find God.
There's no use my going way inside, and staying there,
When so many are still outside and they, as much as I,
Crave to know where the door is.
And all that so many ever find
Is only the wall where a door ought to be.
They creep along the wall like blind people,
With outstretched, groping hands.
Feeling for a door, knowing there must be a door,
Yet they never find it . . .
So I stand by the door.

The most tremendous thing in the world
Is for people to find that door—the door to God.
The most important thing any person can do
Is to take hold of one of those blind, groping hands,
And put it on the latch—the latch that only clicks
And opens to the person's own touch.
People die outside that door, as starving beggars die
On cold nights in cruel cities in the dead of winter
Die for want of what is within their grasp.
They live, on the other side of it—live because they have found it.
Nothing else matters compared to helping them find it,
And open it, and walk in, and find Him . . .

So I stand by the door.
Go in, great saints, go all the way in—
Go way down into the cavernous cellars,
And way up into the spacious attics—
It is a vast roomy house, this house where God is.
Go into the deepest of hidden casements,
Of withdrawal, of silence, of sainthood.
Some must inhabit those inner rooms
And know the depths and heights of God,
And call outside to the rest of us how wonderful it is.

Sometimes I take a deeper look in,
Sometimes venture in a little farther;
But my place seems closer to the opening . . .
So I stand by the door.

There is another reason why I stand here.
Some people get part way in and become afraid
Lest God and the zeal of His house devour them
For God is so very great, and asks all of us.
And these people feel a cosmic claustrophobia,
And want to get out. "Let me out!" they cry,
And the people way inside only terrify them more.
Somebody must be by the door to tell them that they are spoiled
For the old life, they have seen too much:
Once taste God, and nothing but God will do any more.
Somebody must be watching for the frightened
Who seek to sneak out just where they came in,
To tell them how much better it is inside.
The people too far in do not see how near these are
To leaving—preoccupied with the wonder of it all.
Somebody must watch for those who have entered the door,
But would like to run away.
So for them, too, I stand by the door.

I admire the people who go way in.
But I wish they would not forget how it was
Before they got in.
Then they would be able to help

The people who have not yet even found the door,
Or the people who want to run away again from God,
You can go in too deeply, and stay in too long,
And forget the people outside the door.

As for me, I shall take my old accustomed place,
Near enough to God to hear Him, and know He is there,
But not so far from people as not to hear them,
And remember they are there, too.
Where? Outside the door—
Thousands of them, millions of them.
But—more important for me—
One of them, two of them, ten of them,
Whose hands I am intended to put on the latch.
So I shall stand by the door and wait
For those who seek it.
"I had rather be a door-keeper" . . .
So I stand by the door. [4]

I am convinced that men and women who do not know God will respond with open hearts to individuals and churches who express genuine love and care and who demonstrate with their words and actions that they sincerely want to connect.

Try it!

---

4 Samuel Shoemaker, *Extraordinary Living for Ordinary Men* (Grand Rapids: Zondervan, 1966), 139.

Connecting Points

1. Study generational differences.
2. Examine how lost people think. Try to put yourself in their place and mirror their attitudes toward God and the church.
3. Explore the needs of the community. Institute a plan of action, involving people and programs, that will act to meet one need at a time.
4. Study multicultural demographics: who are they, where are they, and how can we connect to them?
5. Cast a missionary vision: Every member is a missionary (not a minister).
6. Create a missionary brigade.
   - Ten bringers who will bring 10 people to church this year.
   - Ten bridgers who will help bridge them into the community through hospitality efforts, welcoming and friendship.
   - Ten builders who will disciple, teach, mentor, dedicate an hour a week to help them develop.
7. Ask yourself: To whom can we open our buildings for community use?
8. Intentionally invite community leaders to come in and share what the community needs and is looking for.
9. Conduct prayer walking and prayer driving events in your city.
10. Don't forget the backsliders.
11. Refuse to maintain a "refuge" mentality.
12. Start small; go slow; watch it grow.
13. Don't hinder the spontaneity of the Holy Spirit with an overemphasis on media and PowerPoint.
14. Refuse to be discouraged. It takes time to train a church to be a missionary outpost.
15. Remember: Relationships rule! God uses relationships to make your church a unique expression of His love on the earth.

Chapter 3

Converting—
The Heart of the Commission

Thus it is written, and thus it was necessary for the Christ to suffer and to rise from the dead the third day, and that repentance and remission of sins should be preached in His name to all nations, beginning at Jerusalem (Luke 24:46, 47).

Paul Conn tells an interesting story from the time he lived in Atlanta some years ago. He found a Yellow Pages listing for a restaurant named "Church of God Grill." Curious, he called the number and inquired about the unusual name.

"We had a mission down here, and we started selling chicken dinners after church on Sunday to help pay the bills," the owner explained. "Well, people liked the chicken, and we did such a good business, that eventually we cut back on the church services. After a while we just closed down the church altogether and kept on serving the chicken dinners. We kept the name we started with, and that's Church of God Grill."[1]

The great challenge of the church is to remember the mission: "That repentance and remission of sins should be preached in His name to all nations." The official denominational Statement of Mission declares, "The mission of the Church of God is to communicate the full gospel of Jesus Christ (Matthew 28:19, 20) in the Spirit and power of Pentecost (Acts 2:1-4, 6, 13-18).[2]

At the heart of the Statement of Vision set forth in the *Minutes of the General Assembly* of the Church of God[3] is this pivotal statement: The Great Commission remains our mandate from Christ. The vision statement is elaborated further in the *Minutes.*

Statement of Vision

Our vision arises from our understanding of what the sovereign God purposes to do for and through His church. The Great Commission remains our mandate from Christ.

The Church of God is to be

1. A movement committed to the authority of Holy Scripture for faith and direction.

---

1 Paul Conn, *Making It Happen* (Old Tappan, New Jersey: Revel, 1981), 75.

2 Dan Black, ed., *Minutes 2008, Church of God Book of Discipline, Church Order, and Governance* (Cleveland, Tenn.: Pathway Press, 2008), 36

3 Black, 37.

2. A fellowship whose worship brings God's power into the life of the church and extends that power through the lives of believers into the marketplace of life.
3. A body that is directed by the Spirit, fully understanding that baptism in the Holy Spirit is both a personal blessing and an endowment of power for witness and service in fulfilling the Great Commission.
4. A people who hunger for God, experience the presence of God, and stand in awe of His holiness as He changes believers into conformity with Christ.
5. A New Testament church that focuses on the local congregation where the pastor nurtures and leads all members to exercise spiritual gifts in ministry.
6. A church that loves all people and stands opposed to any action or policy that discriminates against any group or individual because of race, color, or nationality.
7. A movement that evidences love and concern for the hurts and loneliness of the unsaved through aggressive evangelistic, discipling, and nurturing ministries.
8. A church that is Christ-centered, people-oriented, and need-sensitive in all its programs and ministries.
9. A movement that promotes policies and ministries which reflect an open, sincere effort to remain relevant to each generation.

What a vision! May God help the church to live up to the statement of vision and fulfill Christ's mandate to evangelize the world.

A Challenge to Obey

Can the Great Commission be fulfilled in our lifetime? Many sincere Christians believe that this is not only a possibility, but a probability. Jesus said, "And this gospel of the kingdom will be preached in all the world as a witness to all the nations, and then the end will come" (Matthew 24:14). But can today's church truly carry the gospel of Jesus Christ to the ends of the earth, to all peoples and to all nations? This certainly is what the Lord expected us to do when He commanded the church, "Go into all the world and preach the gospel to every creature. He who believes and is baptized will be saved; but he who does not believe will be condemned" (Mark 16:15, 16). Simply stated, the commission is to "preach the gospel so all will be saved."

God's plan for the church includes preaching the gospel to the whole world, bringing the lost to salvation in Christ, baptizing converts, and teaching them to observe Jesus' commandments.

Can the Great Commission be fulfilled in our lifetime? Many sincere Christians believe that this is not only a possibility, but a probability.

Christians commonly refer to this teaching process as *discipling*. However, discipling cannot begin until *conversion* has occurred. Evangelism—securing converts—is the church's essential activity. While it is possible to evangelize without discipling; it is impossible to disciple without evangelizing. And that is the challenge the church must first meet, for the thrust of the Great Commission is *evangelism*—converting the lost to Christ. Evangelism must be the church's priority.

What Is Meant by *Converted*?

When speaking about making converts, or converting the lost, what is meant by *converted*? Conversion is more than a simple change of mind or a persuasion to a new way of life. Conversion is a supernatural reality that results in a turning away from sin and unbelief in repentance and a turning to Christ in faith and obedience. It does not come through man's intellect or will but through the intervention of the Holy Spirit in the life of an unconverted person.

The conversion process is initiated by the drawing (convicting) of the unconverted individual toward repentance. Jesus said, "No one can come to Me unless the Father who sent Me draws him" (John 6:44). God draws the unconverted through the work of the Holy Spirit. The Spirit's work of conviction makes the unconverted aware of (and convinced of) their sinful condition. "And when He has come, He will convict the world of sin, and of righteousness, and of judgment" (John 16:8).

Once convicted of sin, the unconverted are not hopeless but have the assurance that

> *God so loved the world that He gave His only begotten Son, that whoever believes in Him should not perish but have everlasting life. For God did not send His Son into the world to condemn the world, but that the world through Him might be saved. He who believes in Him is not condemned; but he who does not believe is condemned already, because he has not believed in the name of the only begotten Son of God* (John 3:16-18).

However, true conversion requires repentance. "I tell you, no; but unless you repent you will all likewise perish" (Luke 13:5). But repentance alone is not enough. It must be followed by faith in Jesus Christ and acceptance of Him as Savior. "Believe on the Lord Jesus Christ, and you will be saved" (Acts 16:31). Not only do the convicted have the assurance of God's love, they also have the assurance of Jesus' acceptance when they repent and believe upon Him. "All that the Father gives Me will come to Me, and the one who comes to Me I will by no means cast out" (John 6:37).

To be converted is to be born again—to be changed into a new creation. "Therefore, if anyone *is* in Christ, *he is* a new creation; old things have passed away; behold, all things have become new" (2 Corinthians 5:17). Jesus spoke of the necessity of being born again when he said, "Most assuredly, I say to you, unless one is born again, he cannot see the kingdom of God" (John 3:3). Peter described the effects of this new life in Christ when he wrote, "Since you have purified your souls in obeying the truth through the Spirit in sincere love of the brethren, love one another fervently with a pure heart, having been born again, not of corruptible seed but incorruptible, through the word of God which lives and abides forever" (1 Peter 1:22-23).

This must be the church's message: That God so loved the world that He sent His Son to die for the entire world that all people might have forgiveness of their sins and find new life in Jesus Christ.

Going, converting, discipling, equipping, and empowering are all part of the same mission. It is not complete until it is all done. It is not enough just to announce good tidings. It is not enough just to urge a decision.

The Dimensions of Conversion

Conversion is a miracle. It is described in the Bible by several picturesque words. When the church "dumbs down" the miracle, it fails to pursue a biblical understanding of what happens. It is important for believers to understand these terms. After the first glow of joy and excitement that comes when new converts realize they are now children of God, the question arises, "What has happened in my life?"

One purpose of this chapter is to help explore what it means to become a Christian and to equip believers to better explain to others what happened when Christ comes into a person's heart. People use certain terms to describe their conversion experience and sometimes the terminology is confusing. Some of the key words to help understand conversion are *redemption, justification, reconciliation and regeneration.*

These words are used to describe the process and results of what is commonly called "getting saved." The Bible advises in 1 Peter 3:15: "Always be prepared to give an answer to everyone who asks you to give the reason for the hope that you have" (*NIV*).

Redemption—"I'm Redeemed"

A familiar hymn uses the expression, "I'm redeemed!" A good starting point for understanding what has happened in conversion is this word—*redeemed.* It is commonly used in conversations about pawnshops. Suppose a person who owns an expensive watch discovers he needs money. He takes his watch to a pawnshop. The pawnbroker accepts the watch and gives the man a certain amount of money for it. Along with the money, the pawnbroker also gives him a redemption ticket. The customer may return with the ticket, the amount of money he received from the broker for his watch—plus extra money for interest—and buy back his watch. He can say, "I've redeemed my watch."

In a way, this is what happens in the life of a person who has become a Christian. Man originally belonged to God. Because God created him and loved him, man was related to God—much as a child is related to his father. Instead of obeying God, however, man chose to turn away from Him and live according to his own desires and wishes. Mankind can be considered a rebel against God. "All have sinned and come short of the glory of God" (Romans 3:23).

Man's bad choices separated him even more from God and made him guilty, deserving punishment.

Humanity's sin caused wrong choices in conflict with God's will. Man's bad choices separated him even more from God and made him guilty, deserving punishment. He was unable to pay the price required to make up for his sins. The holiness of God required a perfect man to make up for the badness of all men. God, in His love and mercy, provided One who could pay the price for man's sin. God gave His only Son, Jesus Christ, who came to earth and lived as a man.

Jesus died, even though He was perfectly innocent, so that His death could make amends for the sins of every person.

Do you remember how you felt when you grasped the fact that you were a sinner in the eyes of God? How terrible it was to realize that you had no power to do anything to save yourself! You were hopelessly lost! Then you discovered that Jesus Christ had paid the price you could not pay! You decided that with His help you would turn away from the sin that separated you from God. When you trusted in Him and what He did on your behalf, you were saved.

When believers talk about redemption, they mean that Jesus is the One who paid the price for their sins so that they could once again belong to God. This is what Christ said of His own ministry in Mark 10:45: "For even the Son of Man did not come to be served, but to serve, and to give his life a ransom for many."

Atonement—"I'm Right With God"

Most people have heard sermons urging the hearers to "get right with God." The Bible uses a beautiful word to express what it means to be right in the eyes of God. It appears often in the Old Testament, but only once in the New Testament (KJV). It is the word *atonement*. Actually it is made of three smaller words: *at-one-ment*.

God's plan was for humanity to live in harmony with Him and to enjoy fellowship with Him. But God's holy nature cannot tolerate the presence of sin. Sin has come between God and man and has caused separation.

The good news, according to Romans 5:11, is that "we also joy in God through our Lord Jesus Christ, by whom we have now received the atonement" (KJV). When a person gets saved, he receives "at-one-ment." That is to say, he is no longer separated from the presence of God; he is "at one" with Him. Do you remember how you felt when you realized that you were no longer separated from God? "We . . . joy," the verse says. This means we have reason to be happy. And happiness extends into heaven itself. Luke 15:10 tells us, "There is rejoicing in the presence of the angels of God over one sinner who repents" *(NIV).*

Peace—"I'm at Peace With God"

Along with the feeling of joy and happiness comes a deeper realization that is called peace. *Peace* means "freedom from strife; harmony and concord; an undisturbed state of mind." Paul explains it simply: "We have peace with God through our Lord Jesus Christ" (Romans 5:1).

What Christ did when He paid the price for mankind's sin was break down the dividing barrier that existed between man and God.

A vivid word picture of this peace is found in the Bible. In Ephesians 2, Paul discusses the relationship that existed between Jews and non-Jews during the time of Christ. He pointed out that in the Jewish Temple there was a barrier, a wall beyond which non-Jews could not go. They could not enter the inner recesses of the Temple, the area reserved for the Jewish people. Paul thought of this wall as a symbol of the division that exists between individuals, as well as between men and God. So he said, "For he himself is our peace, who has made the two one and has destroyed the barrier, the dividing wall of hostility" (v. 14, *NIV*). What Christ did when He paid the price for mankind's sin was break down the dividing barrier that existed between man and God.

A person gains peace when he is saved. There is no wall between him and God!

Justification—The Judge Says, "Not Guilty!"

What has happened to the sins committed before a person is saved? According to the Bible, the record is clear; the individual no longer has to answer for those sins.

The word used to describe this happy state of affairs is *justification*. Paul used this term often. The word comes from the Roman court of law and may be illustrated by a woman being brought to court to answer for a crime. Then, for some reason, she does not have to stand trial; she is acquitted. Simply, she is *justified*.

The Word of God says that, as a Christian, the new believer is justified in the presence of God. Because of what Christ has done, she doesn't have to go on trial for those sins. Quite literally, *justification* means "just as if I'd never sinned."

Another good way of thinking of justification is to compare it with forgiveness. The two concepts are related. The difference is that *justification* is more of a legal term, whereas *forgiveness* is a more personal concept. For example, when using the legal term *justification,* one thinks of an accused person being acquitted by a judge; however, when using the more intimate term *forgiveness,* one thinks about pardon being extended by the person who has been offended.

Those who have accepted Christ as Savior will never have to stand before Him when He is judging men to decide if they belong in the kingdom of heaven.

A good discussion of justification in Romans 3:23-26 explains that all men have sinned and come short of what God expects. They need an uprightness they are incapable of producing. But God, through Christ, provides it for them.

Those who have accepted Christ as Savior will never have to stand before Him when He is judging men to decide if they belong in the kingdom of heaven. In His eyes, they are already declared innocent and set free!

Reconciliation—"We're No Longer Enemies"

Have you ever started to discuss a mutual friend's divorce action, only to be told, "Oh, haven't you heard the good news? They have reconciled their differences; they're not getting a divorce." You know what that means. The problem that caused the separation has now been resolved. It has been dealt with and settled and is no longer a factor that will result in divorce.

Reconcile is one of the Bible words that explains what has happened to those who are converted. Its other form, *reconciliation,* means "a renewal of friendship." Those who before were enemies and who had differences that hindered their friendship have resolved those problems and are now friends again. The opposite of *reconcile* is *alienate.* People who cannot, or will not, get along with each other are *alienated.*

Before we were saved, we were alienated from God. Paul describes such people in Ephesians 4:18: "They are darkened in their understanding and separated from the life of God because of the ignorance that is in them due to the hardening of their hearts" (*NIV*). He explains reconciliation in Colossians 1:21, 22: "Once you were alienated from God and were enemies in your minds because of your evil behavior. But now he has reconciled you" (*NIV*).

A convert is no longer an enemy of God, but rather His friend!

Adoption: "I Can Call Him Father"

The clearest picture in the Bible of a sinner who returns to God and is accepted by Him is the story of the prodigal son (Luke 15).

A son asks for his inheritance before his father dies, runs away and wastes all the money. Finally, he returns home broke, hungry, and destitute. His father, who is expected to turn him away, instead welcomes him home and treats him with love, dignity, and respect.

This story illustrates God's eagerness to pardon a repentant sinner. It also teaches another equally meaningful lesson: the intimate Father-son relationship that exists between God and His spiritual children.

One of the words the Bible uses to describe this close relationship is *adoption.* Adoption is a familiar word today. Prospective parents happily welcome a new child into their home and enter into a parent-child relationship just as if the child had been born to them.

Romans 8:15 and 16 explains: "For you did not receive a spirit that makes you a slave again to fear, but you received the Spirit of sonship. And by him we cry, 'Abba, Father'" (*NIV*). *Abba* was an affectionate way of saying "Father" in the language spoken in Paul's day. It is similar to the expression "Daddy" that is used today.

When believers think about all the implications of being able to call God "Father," they realize just how great it is!

It means a great deal to say, "I've been adopted into the family of God." When believers think about all the implications of being able to call God "Father," they realize just how great it is! Perhaps most amazing of all is that, according to the Bible, when individuals become His children, they also become "heirs of God and co-heirs with Christ" (Romans 8:17, *NIV*).

Regeneration—"I've Been Changed"

Perhaps the greatest happiness of the Christian experience comes with the knowledge of being changed. Think about how the Bible pictures the difference in the old life and the new life.

Believers are born again, born from above. They are new creations; they have become pure in heart. They are forgiven; they have been made alive in Christ. All these expressions signal change.

The change takes place by *regeneration*. It might be helpful to think of regeneration as the divine side of what is called *conversion*—a work of God. It is a miracle of God. By an act of His favor, He changes the disposition of the human spirit so that it is renewed in the image of Christ. The sin people once enjoyed now seems awful, and they no longer want to engage in it. Sin no longer dominates the believer's life as it once did. Instead, Christ occupies the center of life.

Believers have been changed! It wasn't the result of turning over a new leaf; it was the result of transforming a life! It didn't come because of wishing and willing; it came because of His great power and His great love. *Regeneration* is just a longer word for what is called the "new birth."

And, There's More!

These are just a few of the ways the Bible talks about the wonderful experience that has occurred in conversion. Other words could be considered, like *substitution* (He took my place), *propitiation* (His sacrifice was sufficient), *imputation* (He put righteousness on my account), and others. Each has shades of meaning that shed light on a different powerful aspect of conversion.

The important truth to grasp is that believers are *saved*! *Saved* is the opposite of *lost*; and "lost" described man's condition before being found by Christ. The Bible emphatically disagrees with universalism, which says that everyone in the world is a child of God. It speaks too clearly of the awful consequences of sin and the separation caused by sin, as well as of the redemptive suffering of Christ, for believers to treat it lightly or to think of His suffering and death as unnecessary.

Christians can now sing with all the saints of God the praise hymn that will be sung to Christ in heaven: "With your blood you purchased men for God from every tribe and nation. You have made them to be a kingdom and priests to serve our God, and they will reign on the earth" (Revelation 5:9, 10, *NIV*).

Christians everywhere can join in the hymn that says:

> *Blessed assurance, Jesus is mine!*
> *O, what a foretaste of glory divine!*
> *Heir of salvation, purchase of God,*
> *Born of His Spirit, washed in His blood.*
> *This is my story, this is my song,*
> *Praising my Saviour all the day long!*
> *—Fanny Crosby*[4]

It is important for the church to develop a Great Commission worldview.

The purpose of *making converts* is to *make disciples.* It is important for the church to develop a Great Commission worldview. Believers can make disciples only after they first make converts, and they cannot make converts unless evangelism is given priority in all the endeavors of the church.

[4] Fanny J. Crosby and Mrs. Joseph F. Knapp, *Church Hymnal* (Cleveland, Tenn.: Church of God Publishing House, 1951), 181.

Conversion must be the heart cry of the church and the all-consuming goal of its ministries. Nothing a believer does is more important than winning the lost to Christ. This lost, troubled world desperately needs the hope and help that can be found only in the true gospel message. The church has the answer for which the world is searching. May God grant us a genuine revival of evangelism in our midst and a new fervency for winning the lost.

Being intentionally sensitive to people and their circumstances and needs will create situations where we can lead them to a life-changing conversion. Jesus illustrated this truth in his encounter with the Samaritan woman (John 4). One of the most interesting details about the meeting is that it is quite likely His disciples passed by the woman on their way into the village. They lacked what so many believers lack: intentional sensitivity. Caught up in personal prejudices and their concern for getting food, they missed the real reason for their detour through Samaria!

During one of the major building projects at Metro Church, I was also leading an emphasis on personal evangelism among our people. A visit to a friend who was pastor of a Baptist congregation, who had recently come through a building project, proved instructive to me. My pastor friend mentioned that while his project was underway, he had won the contractor to the Lord. His testimony prompted me to note that I had not established any relationship—outside the building negotiations—with anyone connected to our project.

I immediately made it my business to get close to the site foreman, with whom I was interacting frequently on building issues. I began praying for him every day. I talked to him about matters other than the construction. One day I learned that his father had died in another state, and I prayed with him for God's comfort. Being quite intentional about it, I looked for times when I could bring spiritual issues into our conversations, always backing my efforts with prayer. After nearly a year of prayer and relationship, the day came when, with just the two of us in the construction trailer, that the Holy Spirit told me, "This is the time." I prayed with him and he was saved.

He lived in a town an hour away, but when the congregation began worshiping in the new sanctuary, he began attending. His wife came with him, and she was converted. Shortly afterwards, his two daughters came to faith.

He had worked with me to design a baptistery with a dividing wall that permitted me to immerse people without having to enter the water with them. Happily, he and his family were among the first to be baptized in the pool he had designed!

Cultivate or Reap?

Everybody likes to reap. Few are happy with the time it takes to cultivate. Reaping is productive and shows instant results. Reaping has the connotation of an ingathering, a return on investment; it is a recompense, or a pleasant result, as in reaping a large profit. People like to reap. The word carries the meaning of "obtaining" or "winning." It seems like every week someone says, "If I win the lottery, here's what I will do with the money." The success of many advertising ventures begins with a letter or e-mail to someone saying, "You are an instant winner!" One of the most successful Internet scams in history begins with a story of millions of dollars in a foreign bank account and how a person can get rich quick with very little effort. Reaping is the end result—the payoff. It is always pleasant and gratifying.

The problem with this line of thinking is that it is impossible to reap without first sowing and cultivating. Cultivating is just plain old hard work. There are always barriers, fences, and obstacles. There is the time factor because it takes time to prepare the soil, buy the seed, plant it, water it, and weed it. This is true whether planting seeds in the ground or launching a new venture in business or ministry.

The word "cultivate" carries the connotation of heavy work, like the following: Prepare, pray, work, labor, plant, plow, care, improve, produce, develop, and devote.

What does all of this mean to the Christian church? It means that if believers want to reap, they are going to have to cultivate. They are going to have to accept the task of understanding the unchurched and learn how to reach them.

It has been well said that the church is the "local branch office" of God's kingdom.

It has been well said that the church is the "local branch office" of God's kingdom. It is the working agency of the Kingdom. As such it exists for a twofold purpose: (1) to demonstrate the Kingdom, and (2) to spread it through obedience to His commands. The job of individual believers is to join the church in accomplishing these two goals.

To succeed, the church needs a plan. Experts say that a firm will grow only as large as its organizational plan allows. A launching point for this to happen is necessary. I suggest that the word **CULTIVATE,** broken down in acrostic form with each letter becoming an action point, will serve that purpose. It would look like this:

Connect through caring and kindness

- Doing deeds of kindness to show people of the love of God

Understand the culture(s)

- Learning where others are coming from in their thinking

Listen to their story

- Taking the time to listen to others to learn about them

Tell your story

- Sharing your personal testimony

Intercede for them

- Offering intercessory prayer for the needs of others

Value relationships

- Cultivating relationships with unsaved people

Answer their questions/ask your questions

- Knowing how to respond to common questions about the Bible, and asking a few of your own

Tell His story

- Presenting a simple way for others to know and understand the gospel

Expect results

- Believing that God will work miracles through His people.

In the following pages, I will discuss each of these points briefly. Because of limited space, I can't go into great detail. The Web page that complements this book, *www.greatcommission.cc,* includes detailed explanations and practical situations for carrying out each aspect of the CULTIVATE approach.

Connect Through Caring and Kindness

All effective evangelism and outreach begins with caring and kindness. Christians are here to help people along the journey, to point them in the right direction. But in the end, it is what God can do for them that makes the difference. People will come to love God and accept Christ through the power of the Holy Spirit that draws them. John says this in his Gospel account: "No one can come to Me unless the Father who sent Me draws him" (John 6:44). The true evangelist is the Holy Spirit. It is the believer's job to present the story in words as well as deeds of action and kindness.

All effective evangelism and outreach begins with caring and kindness.

In this way, evangelism becomes not only something Christ-followers do, but is also a way of life. In Acts 1:8 Jesus said, "Ye shall *be* witnesses unto me." Notice the emphasis is on *being* rather than *doing.* I believe the way others see us living out our Christian life can lead to effective evangelism opportunities. I have often heard the quotation attributed to Saint Francis, "Preach the gospel; use words if you have to."

Eighty-two percent of the unchurched are at least 'somewhat likely' to attend church if they are invited.

In his book, *The Unchurched Next Door,* [5] author Thom Rainer says, "Eighty-two percent of the unchurched are at least 'somewhat likely' to attend church if they are invited." If someone cares enough about people just to befriend them and invite them to church, the majority of them would accept the invitation. I've seen reports that indicate that about 160 million Americans say, "I do not have a born-again experience." If Rainer's research figures are anywhere near accurate, if believers just *invited* people to church, 130 million unchurched people would be willing to attend.

Understand the Culture(s)

This refers to a mind-set or way of thinking. Today's Christians are apt to encounter three groups they must deal with and have a basic understanding of how they think. They are the postmoderns, unbelievers, and cultists.

Postmoderns. Here are some other critical elements that must be considered as the gospel message is shared with them. They value

- Connectivity—They believe no one is isolated

[5] Thomas Rainer, *The Unchurched Next Door* (Grand Rapids: Zondervan, 2008), 141

- Interactivity—The ADHD generation does not like to just sit
- Spirituality—The goal is to unite people of like faith
- Closeness—Relationship matters above all
- Truthfulness—They are all about authenticity
- Impact—They want to change the world
- Imagination—They live in the future, and the future is now
- Relativism—There are no absolutes, including the Bible

With regard to relativism, on a CNBC interview, the late Tim Russert asked Don Imus whether he was a Christian. "Sure, I believe Jesus is the Son of God," Imus responded. "So, you believe you are going to heaven?" Russert asked. "Nah," Imus explained. "I'm into that karma thing."

Oprah Winfrey's personal guru, Marianne Williamson, puts it this way:

> *The word* Christ *is a psychological term. No religion has a monopoly on the truth. Christ refers to the common thread of divine love that is the core and essence of every human being ... Focus on Christ means focus on the goodness and power that lie latent within us, in order to invoke them into realization and expression ... 'I accept the Christ within,' means 'I accept the beauty within me as who I really am.'*[6]

This is classic postmodern thought. Although it is in error, this sort of thing is believed by many in the world.

Unbelievers. As believers share God's message of love with the unchurched, they must overcome some of the

[6] The Quotes of Marianne Williamson, quoted on *www.brainyquotes.com,* accessed July 11, 2009.

unchurched's preconceptions of the Christian community. Nonbelievers don't read the Bible to find out more about God; they watch Christians. Here's what some think of Christians:

1) *Fanatics.* "They're always trying to recruit me," said one woman. "They don't socialize either."

As believers share God's message of love with the unchurched, they must overcome some of the unchurched's preconceptions of the Christian community.

---

2) *Money-driven.* Many non-Christians see money as the main goal of churches and TV evangelists. One man said about Christian television, "They're always pushing and pushing for money."

3) *Wet blankets.* "They don't know how to have fun—they miss out on so much," said one observer.

4) *Judgmental.* "It's supposed to be a religion of love, but they're not loving. They're too busy telling you that their way is right," said one man.

5) *Hypocrites.* An unchurched man said, "Their walk doesn't equal their talk.

Cultists. There are millions of people involved in cultic groups all over the world. They are caught up in a false system of religion. A cult is defined as "a group of people polarized around someone's interpretation of the Bible. It is characterized by major deviation from orthodox Christianity relative to the cardinal doctrines of the Christian faith, particularly the fact that God became man in Jesus Christ."

The glaring difference between cults and mainline Christianity is that every non-Christian cultic system denies that Jesus Christ is God in human form. All cultic systems have some Bible truth, but have some perversion of historic Christian doctrine and theology. The doctrine of the cults in the area of the deity of Christ is the key issue

Listen to Their Story

A great way to begin an evangelism encounter is by taking the time to listen to others to learn about them. Everybody has a story and they are eager to share it. Ultimately, there will be three stories involved in this process: their story, your story, and the central story—the story of Jesus. The next section will deal with equipping believers to tell their story and make it fit into God's greater story—the greatest story ever told.

Listening is sometime difficult for Christians, because when one takes the time to listen to others, he moves away from being the center of attention and invites someone else into that space.

Listening is sometime difficult for Christians, because when one takes the time to listen to others, he moves away from being the center of attention and invites someone else into that space. When a believer genuinely listens to a non-Christian with real concentration and expresses sincere care for their struggles and their pains, something very powerful happens: tensions dissolve, anxieties lessen, and fears diminish. Listening is so simple to do and it's a gift with tremendous healing power that can be offered to others. Let them talk about their past, share their experiences, and express their views. People like to feel that someone is interested in what they have to say and appreciates what they have to contribute. Regrettably, taking time to really listen to what others are saying is very scarce in the Christian community.

Tell Your Story

Your story is your personal testimony. The interrelationship of His story and your story provides the substance of personal witness. Effective witnessing is your telling Jesus' story in a way that is relevant to the listener. Evangelism is all about telling your story—the story of God's generous hospitality in your own experiences. It is the story of God's abundant love in your own corner of the world. Everyone has an exciting testimony!

Your unique experience in coming to Christ can be an effective tool in communicating the gospel to others. A carefully prepared testimony adapts well to either group situations or casual one-on-one conversation. It enables you to speak confidently, knowing that your words are well-chosen, biblically accurate, and appropriate to the situation.

There are three parts to a personal testimony: what your life was like before you received Christ, how you received Christ, and how your life is different as a result of receiving Christ. You should take the time to write it down and practice. A brief version should be prepared. I call this the "napkin version," because you should be able to write all the important parts on a napkin in a restaurant while you are talking with a nonbeliever. Ask the Lord to guide your thoughts and written words. Write as if you were sharing with just one person and your testimony will be more direct. Keep it short. Three minutes (about one and a half to two pages keyboarded, double-spaced) gives you enough time to explain your experience and include a clear presentation of the gospel. That length causes you to be selective about what you communicate.

Here is a working outline:

- Before you received Christ
- How you received Christ
- After you received Christ

Start at a time in life which relates to your experience with Christ. Remember that this is not a biography from childhood. If you became a Christian as a child, but cannot remember making a specific decision to accept Christ, concentrate on describing how Christ has been in your life and the joy that you have received from serving Him. Use language that causes people to really tune in to you. Something like: "Even though my life looked all together, I knew something was lacking."

How has Jesus satisfied your needs that you stated earlier in your presentation?

Next, share about when you first heard the message of Christ and tell about your reaction to it. Tell in plain terms why you made the decision to trust Christ and specifically how you did it. Here in this "How" portion, attempt to present the basics of the gospel clearly and concisely. This may be the only opportunity for a person to know how to become a Christian.

Lastly, share what has happened to you since you became a believer. How has Jesus satisfied your needs that you stated earlier in your presentation? Share about all of the changes that have occurred in your life as a result. Be practical in describing the changes in your life since you became a Christian. Describe how God is helping you learn how to trust Him more. Give examples of ways you have changed, or principles you have discovered in God's Word, and how you have applied them in your daily life. Be sure to mention that you are not perfect now!

Remember that your goal is to explain what Christ has done in your life and to stimulate others to think about their own lives. Do not make your testimony a "preachimony." Leave people with a challenging thought. Keep in mind that they will generally comment on the last thing you say.

Intercede for Them

Someone said, "You can do more than pray after you have prayed. But you cannot do more than pray until you have prayed." Every day, many Christians find themselves working beside people who have never heard a proper presentation of the gospel. Others have heard the gospel but are nowhere near to understanding or accepting it. There is a scriptural mandate to pray for them. In Psalm 2:8 God says,

"Ask of Me, and I will give You the nations for Your inheritance, and the ends of the earth for Your possession." Prayer is the key that opens the eyes of those that do not know the gospel of the love of Christ. Many Christians work a lifetime in secular jobs. This is an advantage for the missionary believer. Imagine what could happen if they all prayed consistently for work colleagues who do not know the Lord.

Value relationships

The famous French painter, Paul Cezanne said, "The relations between objects are more important than the objects themselves." Leonard Sweet, church futurist says, "We're a remote-controlled, security-fenced, Internet-commuting, environmentally-insulated society. We're increasingly cut off from genuine experiences and expressions of community. We're increasingly removed from real, dynamic relationships. Our high divorce rates, our fractured families, our corporate superstructures and our let's-just-move mindset all evidence our failures at relationships." [7]

Often the deepest relationships can be developed during simplest activities. Have you ever wondered what attracted people to the church and ultimately to Christ? A prominent pollster indicates that seven percent of the unchurched plan to attend church this year. Another 33 percent of the unchurched are open to attending church and the thing most likely to attract them is the invitation of a friend. Seventy to ninety percent of all Christians came to know Christ as a

---

[7] Leonard Sweet, "A Sign or a Son?" *http://www.preachingplus.com*, August 3, 2003, p. 6. Accessed July 18, 2009.

result of the influence of a family member or a friend. Just the invitation from a Christian friend can make all the difference for the unchurched.

Often the deepest relationships can be developed during simplest activities.

Missionary believers have to be what we seek to create. It is commonly reported that, in a face-to-face setting,

- 55 percent of the meaning is communicated by the body,
- 38 percent by the tone of voice, and
- only seven percent by the actual spoken words.[8]

Answer Their Questions/Ask Your Questions

People have a right to ask spiritual questions. Sometimes when non-believers ask questions, believers almost feel threatened. Legitimate questions really demand an answer from the Christian community. Through the years, ten questions have been identified that are commonly asked by sincere people. Those who want to deal effectively with non-Christians and lead them to faith will want to learn what these questions are and how they may be answered effectively. The questions and suggested responses are at the Web site, *www.greatcommission.cc.*

[8] Ken Houts, *You Are a Miracle* (Shippenburg, Penn.: Treasure House, 1981), 82

Tell His Story

When Jesus commissioned His disciples to go into all the world and preach the gospel, He did not send them unprepared. They had spent three years observing Jesus' own evangelism methods in dealing with a variety of people.

Christians today can still learn from the examples recorded in the Gospels. The heart of Jesus' ministry was to individuals. While the masses were intrigued by His teachings and miracles, His true followers came through a personal encounter with Jesus Christ, the Living Gospel. Personal evangelism is the art of sharing Jesus passionately.

Christians need to remember that even if the people they talk to don't get saved right away, they have planted a seed.

Personal evangelism is communicating the love of God in Christ to a dying world. In order to reach this postmodern, radical culture for Christ, the church needs to go where people are, and where others will not go. The average Christian today challenges nobody. He can rub shoulders with the world, can meet with unconverted people, and they're no different. Moody Bible Institute took a survey some years ago and found that 95 percent of evangelical believers have never led a soul to Christ. Yet the inflexible precept deeply woven into the commission of the Master is that believers should make disciples of all men.

Christians need to remember that even if the people they talk to don't get saved right away, they have planted a seed.

It is important to have a simple plan of the gospel in mind to share with those who seem ready to hear it. A sample plan is on the Web site that accompanies this book, *www.greatcommission.cc.*

Expect Results

When Christ-followers tell others about Jesus and how much He loves them, that's like planting God's seeds in unbelievers' hearts. When a farmer plants seed, he is confident it will produce a harvest. Most of the time people don't get saved the first time they hear about Jesus. Maybe the first time they heard about Jesus they were not sure they believed in Him. Then later someone else told them about Jesus again, but this time they believed. The Bible says, "I planted, Apollos watered, but God gave the increase" (1 Corinthians 3:6). It is the Holy Spirit who makes the seed grow into salvation. Christians need to remember that even if the people they talk to don't get saved right away, they have planted a seed. Sometimes they might even be watering a seed that someone else has planted. They should not get upset or feel bad because the people they talk to don't get saved right away, but should just keep planting and watering the seeds of God's kingdom and trust the Holy Spirit to make them grow.

The primary goal of preaching should be to proclaim Christ to the lost and to bring them to saving faith in Him.

Outreach to Other Cultures

The community to which today's church reaches out is seldom homogeneous. Up and down the streets live many people who are like the existing members of the church and many people who are different. The church's responsibility is to all of them. Following the Acts 1:8 outline, the New Testament church started among Jews in Jerusalem, but soon reached the Samaritans, the ethnics who lived nearby. Reaching such people is still part of the Great Commission.

As an example of effectiveness in reaching out to cultures other than its own, today's church should take note of Philip's message to the Samaritans, as recorded in Acts 8. Philip preached Christ, which must always be the essence of evangelistic preaching. This message brought about conversion, new life in Christ, and miracles of healing and deliverance from demon possession and sickness. The primary goal of preaching should be to proclaim Christ to the lost and to bring them to saving faith in Him.

Today's church should also take note of Philip's audience. The Judean Jews considered the Samaritans a lowly culture. Samaria was a place the Jews avoided:

> *The tension between the two peoples was so strong that the Jews who traveled between Judea and Galilee usually avoided Samaria by crossing the Jordan and by using the roads on its*

> *eastern bank. Philip's preaching among the Samaritans was, therefore, a surprising action for a Jew. It showed that he had a vision of the possibilities of his message for other peoples than his own.*[9]

Philip was directed to go to the city of Samaria and preach Christ to them. Jesus was there first; the John 4 account of His encounter with the Samaritan woman indicates that He was the first one to reach a Samaritan. In today's world, people groups, like the Samaritans, are looked down upon by other cultures. However, a great harvest of souls awaits the church among these neglected groups. The church that goes to these cultures with the message of Christ and a heart filled with compassion for the lost will surely win many people to the Lord.

While the church in America has traditionally thought of missions in the sense of sending missionaries to remote outreaches of the world, today's reality is that the world has come to America.

Pioneer Church of God missionary to India, Robert F. Cook, began his ministry among the Dalits ("Untouchables" in the caste system of India). He was one of the first Christian leaders to do so, and he won a great harvest among those people for whom no one else cared.

[9] Merrill C. Tenney, *New Testament Survey, Rev.* (Grand Rapids: Eerdmans, 1985), 247.

An Unprecedented Opportunity

While the church in America has traditionally thought of missions in the sense of sending missionaries to remote outreaches of the world, today's reality is that the world has come to America. An unprecedented opportunity awaits the church among the various people groups that have immigrated. The church's reaction to this influx of people groups will have a great effect upon its ability to be a part of fulfilling the Great Commission. Can the church ignore this harvest? Never! The church's focus must be the harvest, not politics.

> *Immigration is quickly changing the ethnic composition of the U.S. population. In 2000, Latinos made up 12.6 percent of the U.S. population; by 2050, they will account for 24.5 percent. Asians in the United States, currently 3.8 percent of the population, will comprise 8 percent by 2050, according to the latest U.S. Census Bureau figures.*[10]

The huge Hispanic influx into America has been the focus of much media attention. Various newspapers, magazines, television commentaries, and talk shows have expounded their particular take on this people movement. On one hand, there are those who are vehemently opposed to immigration and shout, "Close the borders!" On the opposite side are those who cry out for America to continue to be a receiving nation for immigrants who come searching for a better life.

If believers accept the challenge of evangelizing other cultures, what should be the approach? It has been shown that

[10] "55 Trends Facing Tomorrow's World," Special Report from the World Future Society, 7910 Woodmont Avenue, Bethesda, Maryland 20814, 2008.

planting new churches is one of the best ways to evangelize. A good methodology of helping to evangelize people groups is by providing worship opportunities for cultural churches in existing buildings.

A good methodology of helping to evangelize people groups is by providing worship opportunities for cultural churches in existing buildings.

Many congregations across America have already shared the facilities with a worship/evangelistic/celebration service for the people group, a prayer service on a cultural group. The arrangement is almost always a Sunday afternoon or Sunday night weeknight, and an occasional shared service where the people group and the host congregation meet in a joint service.

While these arrangements have sometimes been viewed as the beginning of a multicultural congregation—and indeed led to the establishment of multicultural churches in some situations—in recent years it is more readily apparent that most people groups see such an arrangement as the birthing process of an ethno-centric church for their culture. While the people groups are appreciative of the host congregation's willingness to share their facilities, the groups are looking forward to the day when they will have their own building where they can worship in their own cultural style and setting.

Unfortunately, churches still exist here and there whose people are strongly prejudiced against other cultures. If someone of that persuasion is reading these pages, let me suggest you consider another perspective. Suppose you died and went to heaven, to be greeted there by an angel who shows you your new residence. It is a beautiful place, more elegant than you ever imagined.

Suppose at the same time a brother from another country, culture, or color died and arrived in heaven to be guided by an angel to his new residence, coincidentally across the street from where you will be living. How likely is it that you will approach the angel and protest having to live in heaven near a brother from a different background? Hopefully, not very likely. In a spirit of love and acceptance, churches must stand ready to embrace those who are different and comprise the great harvest the Lord wants to bring in.

The church's approach to evangelizing in other cultures should be the same as that of Philip and the early church. Recognize and celebrate the cultural diversity of people; do not try to change their culture, but accept people for who they are, where they are; and proclaim Jesus to them in the power of the Holy Spirit. Those who embrace the cultural diversity of the church, love people for who they are, and preach Jesus will be effective in evangelizing the immigrant population and will be fulfilling the mandate of the Great Commission to teach all nations.

Converting Points

1. Review the Statement of Vision quoted at the beginning of the chapter. Ask yourself: How well does my church understand why we are here?
2. How would you differentiate between *converting* and *discipling*?
3. What level of theological literacy do you think your church demonstrates? Could your fellow members accurately define such terms as *conversion, redemption, justification, forgiveness, reconciliation, regeneration, adoption*? How could their level of understanding be increased?
4. What does the disagreement between Hebraists and Hellenists ("Grecians and Hebrews") in Acts 6 have to say to us today with regard to our interaction with those of other cultures?
5. Can we think of evangelistic outreach to people here in the United States as "missions," in the same sense as we think of foreign missions? Why or why not?
6. What ethnic groups in the general area of your church might possibly be open to your invitation to start a second congregation using your facilities? How would the other people of the church feel about it?

Chapter 4

Discipling—
The Challenge of the Commission

And Jesus came and spoke to them, saying, "All authority has been given to Me in heaven and on earth. Go therefore and make disciples of all the nations, baptizing them in the name of the Father and of the Son and of the Holy Spirit, teaching them to observe all things that I have commanded you; and lo, I am with you always, even to the end of the age (Matthew 28:18-20).

Discipleship changes the lives of people who have made a determination to follow Christ.

Doug LeRoy, general director of Church of God World Missions, and I were ministering together in Europe recently when he shared this incident.

After the fall of Communism, a great influx of Christians followed. Tremendous evangelistic efforts brought thousands of new converts into the Kingdom.

Doug told me of a conversion with a young woman 10 years later. "Are you still following Christ?" she was asked. "No," she answered. "The Christians told me God loved me. They said God had a plan for me. But they never told me who God is. The Bahá'í people came afterward and told me who God is. I am now a follower of the Bahá'í faith."

It is not enough to evangelize people. The church must also disciple them.

During his earthly ministry, Christ made "making disciples" a priority. He poured Himself into the disciples and taught them vital lessons to fulfill God's plan of new life and abundant life, and to "make disciples" after He was gone.

As 21st-century disciples, believers are to embrace the same admonition that Christ gave to the first-century disciples. They were faithful in fulfilling the instructions and modeled His reaching, teaching, and training characteristics as a lifestyle.

What Is a Disciple?

What is a disciple? Mark 3:13-15 perhaps summarizes it best, "He went up to the mountain and summoned those whom He Himself wanted, and they came to Him. And He appointed the twelve, that they might be with Him, and that He might send them out to preach, and to have authority to cast out demons." In that sense a disciple is someone who is deeply and personally committed to Jesus Christ by faith, who binds himself to Him to learn how to manifest His power and authority and continue His work.

Discipleship must be viewed in terms of a relationship instead of rules and regulations.

Discipleship must be viewed in terms of a relationship instead of rules and regulations. Focusing on rules leads to legalism and religion. Jesus wants more than that. He wants relationship. Just as Jesus in Galilee called certain men to be with Him and follow Him, so believers today have been summoned by Him as well.

George Barna[1] lists the marks of a disciple as:

- Disciples experience a changed future through their acceptance of Jesus Christ as Savior and of the Christian faith as their defining philosophy of life.
- Disciples undergo a changed lifestyle that is manifested through Christ-oriented values, goals, perspectives, activities and relationships.
- Disciples mature into a changed worldview, attributable to a deeper comprehension of the true meaning and impact of Christianity. Truth becomes an entirely God-driven reality to a disciple. Pursuing the truths of God becomes the disciple's lifelong quest.

The marks are the church's portrait of a disciple and definition of spiritual maturity.

---

1 George Barna, *Growing True Disciples* (Ventura, Calif.: Issachar Resources, 2000) 26.

Will Mancini in his book, *Church Unique*[2], reminds the church that the mission is what is measured. He describes the set of attributes in an individual's life that define or reflect the accomplishment of the church's mission as "marks." The marks are the church's portrait of a disciple and definition of spiritual maturity. Marks supply the standard by which the mission can be measured with respect to an individual's development through the ministry of the church. He goes on to say, "Marks create the definition of a disciple, correct a knowledge-centered spirituality, and constitute the foundation for systematic teaching." The church must help people identify marks as the mental framework for them to catch and digest truth.

A man was known as a* mathetes *or disciple when he bound himself to another in order to acquire his practical and theoretical knowledge.

It is vitally important to establish the right kind of marks for discipleship. Mancini recounts the story of an Olympic marksman who was one rifle-shot away from winning a medal. He took careful aim and centered the bullet in the heart of the bull's-eye. Unfortunately, however, he was in Lane 2, and the target he fired at was in Lane 3. He missed out on the medal completely, because he fired at the wrong target.

His story reminds me of a farmer whose house, barn, outhouse and every other building was dotted with bull's-eyes.

2 Will Mancini, *Church Unique* (San Francisco: Jossey-Bass, 2008), 152.

They appeared high and low, on all sides of the buildings. Remarkably, every target was centered with the mark where a bullet had pierced its center. "How is it possible that you hit dead center of every target?" he was asked. "Oh, that's easy," he responded, "I shoot first, then paint the target!"

Defining a Disciple

The Greek term *mathetes* refers generally to any "student, pupil, apprentice, or adherent," as opposed to a "teacher." The verb was used to denote the process by which one acquired theoretical knowledge. A disciple was a learner. A man was known as a *mathetes* or disciple when he bound himself to another in order to acquire his practical and theoretical knowledge. In the ancient world, *mathetes* was most often associated with people who were devoted followers of a great religious leader or teacher of philosophy. Several traditions within the national life of Israel make it reasonable to assume that the concept and practice of personal discipleship existed in their culture. Even in the home, as traditions were passed down through events such as Passover, the parents were providing a form of discipleship. When God delivered His people, and altars were subsequently built, they were used as a part of the discipleship process in the individuals. Parents understood their role to be that of disciplers of their children within the home.

In general, the education of boys in first century Judaism centered in the home around Torah learning. The content of the Torah, essentially the first five books of the Old Testament, was taught primarily by the father. But during the time of Jesus, evidence suggests that primary schools had been developed to mitigate against the inroads of foreign influence. After a boy reached 13 years of age, there was usually not more formal education. If he wanted further training in preparation for being a judge, teacher, scribe or head of a synagogue, he might seek to study as a disciple under a specific scholar, learning to imitate his life and faith and concentrating on mastering the Mosaic Law as well as the traditional interpretations of it.

The apostle Paul was an example of a Jewish boy who had left home (i.e., Tarsus) to study the Law under Gamaliel, a famous rabbi in Jerusalem (Acts 5:34; 22:3). The Pharisees had devised a system in which they had codified the Mosaic Law into prohibitions and commandments. They required those who followed them to submit to their interpretations of this Law. Because the Pharisees considered themselves the official interpreters of the Law, they promoted themselves to positions of authority in Israel.

Making Disciples

"Making disciples" was the dominant priority when I was a pastor. I knew pleasing the Lord and numerical church growth rested on the premise of guiding individuals in becoming mature followers of Jesus Christ—dedicated, devoted, determined disciples. Let me share concepts and materials that I utilized in my pastoral ministry and found helpful in developing disciples.

The Bible refers to a believer, a disciple, as a **saint**. In making disciples, a commitment must be made by the church to developing the saintly characteristics in every believer.

S —**Saved** by grace (saved and baptized)

A —**Anointed** by the Holy Spirit for ministry (Spirit-filled and serving)

I —**Instructed** in the Bible (discipled and equipped)

N —**Nurtured** by fellowship (sharing and caring)

T —**Tells** others about Christ (investing and inviting)

These saintly characteristics are manifested in 12 distinct ways. A disciple is . . .

1. Teachable—Proverbs 9:8-10; Matthew 4:19
2. In love with Jesus supremely and submitted to His lordship—John 3:16, 17
3. Committed to a life of personal purity—Proverbs 8:13.
4. Committed to grow by developing a daily devotional life—Mark 1:35.
5. Developing the practice of a dynamic study of the Bible—John 8:31, 32.
6. Committed to a lifestyle of personal evangelism—Acts 1:8.
7. Committed to the worship of Almighty God—John 4:20-26.
8. Devoted to Christian fellowship—Acts 2:42, 44-46.
9. Responsible as a faithful steward—Luke 16:10.
10. Committed to accept and assert spiritual authority—Luke 10:19, 20.

11. Willing to unwrap and utilize spiritual gifts—1 Corinthians 12:1-6.
12. A minister (missionary) of Jesus Christ—Ephesians 4:11, 12.

Beginning the Discipleship Process

Developing disciples has many facets. In Christian families, it begins in the home with parents. Then the church plays a major role with discipleship ministries for children, youth, young adults, and adults. Neglect in any one of these areas has serious repercussions. That is why balanced Kingdom development is essential in the process of growing disciples.

When all aspects of God's plan for His people and church are understood and embraced, matured, fully developed followers of Christ will be the result.

From a pastor's perspective, I want to emphasize the values of a New Believer's Class. This touches every aspect of discipleship—personal spiritual growth, the mission of the church, parenting, giving and serving. When all aspects of God's plan for His people and church are understood and embraced, matured, fully developed followers of Christ will be the result.

Setting the Stage for Discipleship Training

Highlight Water Baptism. Part of the Great Commission is "baptize them." Why did Jesus emphasize this as part of His command? Water baptism is a public profession of faith and a symbol of immersion in the body of Christ. It is a vital part of the discipleship process.

Despite the specific instructions of the Lord, however, the church seems not to take baptism seriously. For example, records indicate that last year the Church of God in the U.S. reported 251,303 saved and only 35,387 baptized in water.[3] This means for every 100 persons reported saved, only 14 of them were baptized.

Water baptism was one of my most enjoyable duties as a pastor. I made it a special celebration for the family, their relatives and friends. Here are some ideas to help make baptism an unforgettable observance.

1. Teach a class on the subject, "The Meaning of Water Baptism."
2. Provide invitation cards to families to mail to relatives and friends.
3. Reserve seating for family and guests. They are recognized by name and relationship.
4. Provide a certificate and video of the baptismal service.
5. Plan a reception following the service to meet the pastoral staff.
6. Take a photo of the individual who was baptized with his/her relatives and friends.
7. Have the person who led the nonbeliever to Christ to share a testimony.

To be baptized in water in the presence of fellow Christians provides a great opportunity for a believer to

[3] The data comes from the 2008 Statistical Report in the Church of God Office of Business and Records.

publicly renounce sin in his life, to allow himself to put to death all the wrong stuff as he is buried with Christ and raised to newness of life. To make this a celebration gives it the honor Jesus does.

Pastor Tom Sterbens sees the passage of the Israelites through the Red Sea after their deliverance from Egyptian bondage as prefiguring water baptism, referring to the 1 Corinthians 10:2 passage. When he performs baptisms, he quotes the verses that describe the complete devastation of the pursuing Egyptian army in the waters, "They were seen no more," as an assurance to the ones being baptized that whatever was pursuing them, whatever was attempting to thwart their deliverance and victory, would be washed away in the waters of baptism. It's a great and encouraging thought!

It is interesting to note various cult groups and world religions whose followers are devout in their faith and commitment. Muslims pray five times a day, wherever they are. While walking through Times Square in New York, it is not uncommon to see a Muslim unroll his prayer rug and bow in prayer. It is a challenge for Pentecostals to perform a self-evaluation and discover the depth of our discipleship commitment. In a day when people are looking for something to commit their lives to, wholeheartedly offering themselves for a cause, church leaders must direct them in their search.

Many years ago in Second Baptist Church of Cincinnati, Ohio, the pastor led in a foreign missions service and concluded by inviting the worshipers to respond with a faith promise pledge indicating how much they would give to missions in the next year.[4] When the ushers were going through the cards later, they found one signed by a 12-year-old boy. He had written in soft-lead pencil, "I have no money; I give myself."

A little over eight years later, that same church and pastor conducted a commissioning service to send out a young man who would be one of the first American Protestant missionaries in China. He was I.P. Shook, the same person who, years before, had written, "I give myself." God is still looking for people who will make that kind of commitment.

A mistake commonly made by churches is thinking that getting a new convert "plugged in" to a ministry of the church is the way to ensure success in discipleship. I have learned by experience that discipleship is best processed by personal Bible study, prayer, a discipling relationship, and the stewardship of time, talent, and treasure. It should not be surprising to any believer that Jesus got it right: "Teaching them to observe all things I have commanded you."

Discipleship for All Ages

Infant Dedication. To support the idea that discipleship begins at a young age, more attention should be paid to baby dedication. This signifies the relational importance and the

---

[4] This moving story was recounted by Paul L. Walker in a sermon I heard some years ago.

vitality of the community during the dedication of infants or children.

The dedication service can provide opportunities for illustrating and exhorting the family of God to be involved in the process of discipleship in the child's life.

One idea is to have the age group leader for each age group of the church participate during the act of dedication. Symbolically, each age group leader could pass a baton to the next age group leader, making a statement of commitment to the individual being dedicated during the years they are present in their respective ministries. This would demonstrate unity of purpose to the congregation and to the parents. Inviting family and friends of the parents of the child will also provide them with the opportunity to see the commitment of the congregation to relational discipleship.

Children's Ministries. Churches serious about discipleship understand that effective training begins with children as soon as they are born. They create a plan that will take the infant through a continuing discipleship strategy as he grows. Many churches historically invest their money in ministering to adults. Budgets often are restricted with regard to children. However, if churches were to objectively evaluate where they will get the greatest return on investment, they would instead devote resources to ministries for children. Proverbs declares that if parents will train up a child in the way he should go, when he is old he will not depart from it (see Proverbs 22:6).

Discipleship Points

I think of discipleship in this way: it must be sought, taught, caught, and brought.

Discipleship must be sought. Although the church bears the weight of responsibility for training converts in the ways of God, discipleship cannot happen if the new believer does not desire it strongly in his life. One must actively seek to be a disciple.

Discipleship must be taught. Many years ago a statesman who had attended Williams College when the renowned educator, Mark Hopkins, was president defined the ideal education as "Mark Hopkins on one end of the log and a student on the other end." Discipleship depends on an effective teacher.

Discipleship must be caught. Unless a church catches a vision of discipling its people, it will not happen.

Discipleship must be brought. Leaders must bring discipleship thinking, tools and methods to the scene. Disciples must not only believe in Jesus, but they must also believe that discipleship is the way to grow in Christ.

Discipleship is developmental, as may be observed as follows:

- Discipleship is *invitational.* The hungry-hearted new Christian must be invited into a discipleship bond with someone who cares about him.
- Discipleship is *instructional.* There must be teaching.
- Discipleship is *relational.* Relationships with mature believers who are willing to invest in the growth of the learner is necessary.

- Discipleship is *processional.* It requires more than a four-week sermon series or 10 mid-week lessons to produce a disciple.
- Discipleship is *continual.* It is a lifelong process requiring lifelong learning.
- Discipleship is *confrontational.* A teachable spirit on the part of the disciple is necessary, which gives permission to be confronted when false assumptions or immature behavior are apparent.
- Discipleship is *personal.* Disciples are not mass-produced. They are developed over time through teaching and learning, opportunities and challenges, hills and valleys.

Effective churches make discipleship a priority. They develop a culture where discipleship is not only encouraged but expected. When people are saved, they should be given a roadmap for discipleship. It could look like this:

A Discipleship Roadmap

- The new birth is experienced.
- The convert is baptized in water.
- A new believer's class is offered.
- Characteristics of a disciple are explained.
- A personal spiritual coach is adopted.
- Regular meetings with a coach/mentor take place over a period of time. Question and answer sessions explore progress.
- The disciple begins discipling others.

What's a Disciple To Do?

The Great Commission essentially outlines what Jesus expected the Twelve and others who followed them to do after He returned to heaven. It is interesting to note that in Greek, the only specific command verb in Matthew 28:19-20 is "Make disciples."

The Great Commission instructs Christians to make disciples while they are going throughout the world. How? By baptizing and teaching them all that Jesus commanded. *"Make disciples"* is the command. "Baptizing" and "teaching" are the means by which they fulfill the "make disciples" aspect of the Great Commission.

In the Great Commission, the Lord exhorts the church to do the job of world evangelization. Some people focus on that part of the Great Commission primarily as the basis for world missions. It is right to focus on the evangelization aspect, but one must not miss the command of Christ to *build disciples.* Everything believers do as the body of Christ should revolve around the discipleship process. If they want to be truly missional, it will require that they understand the necessity of helping Christ-followers realize that their commitment to Christ is a lifestyle and that lifestyle demands discipleship.

It is right to focus on the evangelization aspect, but one must not miss the command of Christ to *build disciples.*

The Barna survey[5] of the state of discipleship in the American church mentioned earlier in this chapter regarded the spiritual lives of adults and teenagers who have made a personal commitment to Jesus Christ identified a shallowness of their faith. Some of the markers that reveal this are . . .

- When Christian adults were asked to identify their most important goal for their life, not a single person said it was to be a committed follower of Jesus Christ, or to make disciples of Christ.
- Less than one out of every five born again adults had any specific and measurable goals related to their personal spiritual development.
- Less than one percent of all believers perceived a connection between their efforts to worship God and their development as disciples of Jesus.
- A minority of adult and teen believers contends that absolute moral truth exists.
- Less than one out of every 10 believers possesses a biblical worldview as the basis of his/her decision-making or behavior.
- When given 13 basic teachings from the Bible, only one percent of adult believers firmly embraced all 13 as being biblical perspectives.

Less than one out of every 10 believers possesses a biblical worldview as the basis of his/her decision-making or behavior.

---

[5] Barna, 31-40.

Churches that do a good job of disciple-making focus not only in the mastery of Bible knowledge, making content-sharing the primary goal, but also have majored in the development of character. They understand that discipleship is not only taught in an academic manner, but is caught through a transformational lifestyle and example.

New Testament Examples

Paul's life and work show us that it is possible to follow Christ's example. He imitated the example of Jesus. After his conversion and after being discipled, he proceeded with an effective and powerful ministry. His work did not begin immediately, however. It is likely that Paul went through years of discipleship, possibly as many as 16, before he initiated his first missionary journey.[6] During the years of his ministry, more than 25 individuals are mentioned as having been his companions, essentially his disciples. Many of them accomplished much for the kingdom. After reading about Paul's missionary journeys and what he and his coworkers accomplished, it is possible to realize that believers today can impact the world.

The Book of Acts reveals many examples of people who were committed to both being disciples and producing disciples of Christ. Even those with deficiencies in their life, like Peter, show that it is still possible to serve the Lord and make an impact. The story of Stephen inspires and motivates believers to coach or mentor someone else. These were individuals just like 21st-century Christians, yet they were

---

[6] J.B. Lightfoot, *The Epistle of Paul to the Galatians* (Grand Rapids: Zondervan, 1981) 124.

disciples of Christ and because of their zeal and passion made such an impact that their stories are still being told.

Discipleship Is a Community Affair

Discipleship is relational. By uniting our lives in Christ's, we are united with God. Discipleship by its very nature is about Jesus and the pursuit of humanity to be more like Christ.

What is it like to be created in the image of God? Ephesians 4:24 says we are to be righteous, holy and true. That is what we strive for because that is what God is like. It is following Jesus down a path of self-denial, forsaking possessions and bearing a cross. Disciples are to become like Jesus, do the works of Jesus, proclaim the words of Jesus, publicly confess Jesus, and overcome like Jesus. It is about knowing God. It is about authentic transformation.

Discipleship is a vertical relationship, upwards toward Christ. It is also a horizontal relationship. The Book of Acts demonstrates the communal aspect of discipleship. It is nurtured by others. It includes coaching and mentoring. It really is a "family affair." Discipleship cannot occur in a vacuum. It happens within the community of faith, with other believers who are willing to coach, guide, direct, and encourage. Disciples cannot reach their full potential unless they are part of a body that is like-minded in faith and purpose.

In Bible days, disciples would find a rabbi whom they would like to follow, or "come underneath their yoke." The rabbi would accept them and they would spend the rest of their days learning the ways of the rabbi. These disciples

(Talmidims) would leave everything behind and seek to be like the rabbi. They were exhorted to "cover yourself with the dust of your rabbi's feet." That signified following the rabbi closely, going where the rabbi went, learning from him, in such a close proximity that they would get the dust of the rabbi on their feet. It was about action; it required that they "do something."

Coaching and mentoring are seen as invaluable in the discipleship process. This carries with it an accountability for the discipler to be authentic. This mentoring process takes place as we watch, listen, serve, follow, learn, read, glean, and emulate. It is the way of Christ. Paul said, "Follow me, as I follow Christ" (1 Corinthians 11:1).

This mentoring process takes place as we watch, listen, serve, follow, learn, read, glean, and emulate. It is the way of Christ.

Paul's life exemplifies the roles of mentoring and coaching. He was mentored by believers such as Barnabas. He had friends and companions like Silas, for example. He mentored young believers like Timothy. That is the way of discipleship. It is not done in isolation. Humans were created to be with others. In fact, they cannot function well, for a very long period of time, without others.

The type of relational commitment to Jesus that is needed is be exemplified by an African pastor in Zimbabwe in writings found among his things after he was martyred.[7]

> *I am a part of the fellowship of the unashamed. The die has been cast. I have stepped over the line. The decision has been made. I am a disciple of His and I won't look back, let up, slow down, back away or be still. My past is redeemed. My present makes sense. My future is secure. I'm done and finished with low living, sight walking, small planning, smooth knees, colorless dreams, tamed visions, mundane talking, cheap living and dwarfed goals. I no longer need preeminence, prosperity, position, promotions, plaudits or popularity. I don't have to be right, or first, or tops, or recognized, or praised or rewarded. I live by faith, lean on His presence, walk by patience, lift by prayer and labor by Holy Spirit power. My face is set. My gait is fast. My goal is heaven. My road may be narrow, my way rough, my companions few, but my guide is reliable and my mission is clear. I will not be bought, compromised, detoured, lured away, turned back, deluded or delayed. I will not flinch in the face of sacrifice or hesitate in the presence of the adversary. I will not negotiate at the table of the enemy, ponder at the pool of popularity, or meander in the maze of mediocrity. I won't give up, shut up or let up until I have stayed up, stored up, prayed up, paid up and preached up for the cause of Christ. I am a disciple of Jesus. I must give until I drop, preach until all know and work until He comes. And when He does come for His own, He'll have no problems recognizing me. My colors will be clear!*

Following their evaluation that showed the lack of spiritual formation among many of their members, Willow Creek Association published the results of an extensive sur-

7 This statement has been widely published, sometimes attributed to Robert Moorehead, other times to the unknown African pastor. It is not certain who originally wrote it, but the power of its declaration is apparent.

vey of their church ministries.[8] This text illustrates what Willow Creek calls the "unfinished symphony" lifestyle, a four-stage spiritual growth continuum—moving from exploring Christ until arrival as Christ-centered—and the attitudes and beliefs that help people move from one stage to another.

Because discipleship is not an instantaneous act, there must be time for Christ-followers to develop before being immersed in service and given positions of authority and leadership.

Because discipleship is not an instantaneous act, there must be time for Christ-followers to develop before being immersed in service and given positions of authority and leadership. Premature offering of positions and authority may lead to bad decision-making and subsequent failure. The church's goal is not filling positions, but building disciples, helping them recognize and develop their individual and unique gifts and callings. Rather than writing down a list of positions in the church, perhaps it would be better to write down the people's names in the church, along with their gifts and talents. Then, believers can determine what God wants the church to do in the community based on what and who He has given it to work with. That is the way to build disciples.

---

8 Greg Hawkins and Cally Parkinson, *Follow Me* (Chicago: Willow Creek Resources, 2008).

The disciples Jesus trained walked and talked with Him 24/7. The methodology He used provides an example for believers today and also gives insight as to the process involved in building disciples. The church must understand that discipleship is its purpose. And, if Christians are indeed going to win the world and fulfill their mission, the only way to accomplish it is by building disciples!

Small Groups

Realizing the power of community in learning, effective churches utilize small groups. But the purpose of small groups is not just to cover curriculum. Effective small groups allow people to declare to each other what is going on in their lives, what they would like to see going on in their lives, and what kind of help and accountability they need to move toward their hopes and away from their frustrations. This brings life to the table.

Excellent resources are on the market, but they must be seen as tools to assist in the building of community, not the focus. A number of effective churches have developed successful small group ministries. In the Internet companion to this book, *www.greatcommission.cc*, I have listed information and resources from some of them.

Ana Rut Diaz, the pastor of the Oasis of Love Church of God in Tegucigalpa, Honduras, has developed a congregation of more than 6,000 building on the concept of growth through small groups. She credits the small group emphasis for the phenomenal increases the church has seen. Many of the large churches in Indonesia, reaching many thousands, depend on small groups to provide effective pastoral care.

I am convinced that small groups work best when they are viewed not as appendages to other church programs, but as a vital part of church life.

One of Jesus' first acts when He began his public ministry was to form a small group.

Good Web sites for small group resources include *www.buildingsmallgroups.com*, and *www.smallgroupministry.com*.

Each of these models understands the example of Jesus. One of Jesus' first acts when He began his public ministry was to form a small group. Mark's gospel states, "He appointed twelve, designating them apostles, that they might be with him and that he might send them out to preach and to have authority to drive out demons" (Mark 3:14, 15). He carried out his public ministry in the context of a small group. He spent three years with them in close fellowship. He asked them to join the group because He wanted their support and encouragement. He wanted them to team with Him in ministry. And, in discipling them, He also wanted to establish a model for generations to come as the context in which believers live out their journey of faith.

Personal Development Plan

A model that provides a tool for measuring growth of individuals includes a Personal Development Plan. Individuals, who are part of a small group strategy, determine what they need to focus on and what they will be doing during a specific time period. They look at what the church has to offer and select resources for reading and activities. Finally, they pull the personal plan together and share it with others in the small group to provide accountability. This also provides support and encouragement while individuals are working on the areas of need in their discipleship process.

Pastor Johnny Moore leads a church in the rural community of Cairo, Georgia. He has been using this approach at the Church of God Family Worship Center for several years and has found it to be helpful in building people. Each month, he selects a book he believes will be beneficial for those involved in the plan.

By being proactive in providing resources for the Christ-followers in their churches leaders can assist individuals in their spiritual growth and maturity. The Personal Development Plan will need to be based on the definition of what it means to be a disciple.

Whatever the methodology chosen by church leaders, let your target for discipleship be the production of *saints*!

DISCIPLING POINTS

1. As a church, study and define the characteristics of a disciple. Then, help each Christ-follower to identify areas where he/she needs to concentrate during a designated period of time. Assist with creation of a Personal Development Plan. Set up a strategy that will provide tools and resources for individuals who choose to participate.
2. Evaluate the infant dedication process. What could be done differently to signify the importance of this activity and what steps will be taken to make it more effective?
3. What could be added to the water baptism process that would make it a greater tool for the discipleship process?
4. What are the marks, core beliefs, practices and virtues of your church and ministry? Identify them. What makes your church unique in your community? Identify what God has called your church to be and do. Identify what your church is aiming for with reference to the building of disciples. How do you know when you have made a disciple? What is the target you are aiming for?
5. Evaluate your church's community structure. How is the church providing opportunities for community building? How are you involving others outside your community of faith in those small groups?
6. Gather the leaders of your church together and ask the tough questions:
    - Is the church building people, making disciples?
    - How is the church helping people identify their gifts and talents and then assisting them with getting involved in ministry?
    - As the church focuses on discipleship as a core element, are there ministries that need to be dropped or revised that are not presently supporting the goal of making disciples?
    - How is the church helping people identify their gifts and talents and then assisting them with getting involved in ministry?

Chapter 5

Equipping—
The Task of the Commission

So Jesus said to them again, "Peace to you! As the Father has sent Me, I also send you." And when He had said this, He breathed on them, and said to them, "Receive the Holy Spirit. (John 20:21-23).

Tourists in San José, California, visit what is called the Winchester Mystery House[1], built over a 38-year period beginning in 1884 by the widow of the famed Winchester repeating rifle manufacturer. Sarah Winchester had been told by a spiritualist, following the death of her child and her husband, that the spirits of all those killed by the famous

---

1 Lisa Selby, *The Inscrutable Mrs. Winchester and Her Mysterious Mansion* (Frederick, Maryland: PublishAmerica, 2006).

rifle would haunt her the rest of her life, and the only way she could avoid the spirits would be to build a house and continue its building until her death.

The result of the strange advice is a 160-room mansion with stairs that go up to the ceiling rather than to the next floor, skylights in the floors looking to rooms below, glass doors to bathrooms, fireplaces whose chimneys go only to the ceiling and scores of other oddities. Some rooms are walled up, surrounded by other rooms. Mrs. Winchester managed to keep 22 carpenters employed on a daily basis for nearly four decades.

The Winchester Mystery House, with its wandering corridors and senseless design, may be a good illustration of a church that boasts a lot of activity, but whose ultimate achievement is something other than fulfilling the Great Commission.

Losing Direction

In the year A.D. 313, things began to change in the church. Some of it was good. Most of it wasn't.

This dramatic event would eventually lead to Constantine's alleged conversion to the Christian religion, and in 313 he would decree the Edict of Milan.

Before A.D. 313, Christianity was a persecuted faith. The previous 10 years (303-313) were horrific. The Roman Emperor Diocletian ordered the destruction of Christian scriptures and churches, prohibited Christians from assembling for worship, and rescinded all legal rights for Christians. Pastors and bishops were demanded to perform pagan sacrifices. Thousands were martyred, and thousands more were imprisoned.

This dramatic event would eventually lead to Constantine's alleged conversion to the Christian religion, and in 313, he would decree the Edict of Milan.

But all that changed in A.D. 313 under the new emperor, Constantine. According to tradition, he saw in a vision the sign of the cross in the sky with these words, *in hoc signo vinces,* meaning "conquer by this sign." The shields of his soldiers overnight were inscribed with the emblem of the cross, and they easily won their next battle. This dramatic event would eventually lead to Constantine's alleged conversion to the Christian religion, and in 313, he would decree the Edict of Milan. This decree made Christianity a legal religion. It legitimized Christianity, essentially elevating it to the preferred religion of the empire. Rapidly, the percentage of Christians in the empire went from less than 10 percent to an overwhelming majority—without a single conversion!

There was no more need to evangelize. There was no more need to plant churches. Everyone was a "Christian." The Great Commission was "fulfilled." The wheels of the church, the great gospel chariot, fell off. A church that had been a great spiritual force became an audience almost overnight.

No longer a missional body, the church slipped into a maintenance mode. It lost its ability to be salt and light. Within three centuries, the church would lead Western Europe into the Dark Ages.

It would not be until almost 1,200 years later that the Reformers would initiate spiritual renewal and bring a level of vitality back to the church.

It would not be until almost 1,200 years later that the Reformers would initiate spiritual renewal and bring a level of vitality back to the church. The priesthood of every believer was a cardinal doctrine of the Reformation. Martin Luther felt that the disintegration of church structure into a "clergy-dependent/congregation-passive" model was clearly nonbiblical. He made his views very clear when he wrote, "Through baptism all of us are consecrated to the priesthood. . . . For whoever comes out of the water of baptism can boast that he is already consecrated priest, bishop and pope."[2] However, despite the Reformation's emphasis on the priesthood of the believer, the church still struggles to find meaningful strategies to implement this New Testament ideal. The post-Constantine model still dominates, especially in North America. Church still resembles and functions much like an audience. What do most people visualize when they hear the word "church"? A building, a pastor speaking from a pulpit, a choir or a praise team singing, all this to

---

2 *The Babylonian Captivity of the Church: The Works of Martin Luther* (Minneapolis: Augsburg Fortress Press, 1990).

people sitting in rigid rows of pews. It is more a performance than a force, more an audience than an army.

Reprogram the Church

How many weekly hours can truly be expected of a highly committed Christian to dedicate to church activities—what are called church programs? In smaller towns and rural areas, one might expect four to six hours a week. In cities, where people spend hours in long commutes, the number would be less—maybe four hours maximum. Remember, this is not about living a consistent Christian life. That's a lifestyle commitment, and it is 24/7. This discussion is talking about church programs.

How many weekly hours can truly be expected of a highly committed Christian to dedicate to church activities—what are called church programs?

Now, consider how these valuable hours will be utilized. Traditionally, the church wants involvement in a Sunday school program and morning worship. That's three of the hours. Sunday night service—that's another hour and a half, and, of course, there is the mid-week service—another hour. Many churches are programmed in such a way that the four to six hours people can give are consumed with creating various audience venues. These are venues that can easily be produced and maintained by about 15 to 20 percent of the congregation. So what are the other 80 percent doing? They are an audience—the church of today hasn't moved far from the post-Constantine model.

No matter how much leaders preach about people getting involved, and filling the altars with people making commitments to serve Christ, the structure and schedule must change before people are released. Churches have to reduce "audience time" and increase intentional missional programming. Some of the preaching events may need to go so other gifts may be expressed through the church. How many sermons and lectures each week do people really need to hear? On the other hand, how many opportunities for serving, building community, and outreach do churches need to build into the church calendar?

The places around the world where revival is occurring are places where Christians are thinking and living as a force, not an audience.

The places around the world where revival is occurring are places where Christians are thinking and living as a force, not an audience. Pastors and church leaders are training people to preach the gospel, to pray for the sick, to cast out evil spirits, to care for the poor and the broken, to build bridges to the unchurched. In other words, they are equipping the people to do the work of the ministry. It's a New Testament model that must be rediscovered in the 21st-century American church.

The Reformation restored the doctrine of the priesthood of the believers theoretically. The church of today must restore it in practice. Has the time come? Will it occur in this century? Will a missional church arise?

Shift to an Equipping Model

The traditional church model operates from an institutional paradigm. This could be thought of as the "clergy-dependent model." In this model, pastors do the ministry, while God's people are the recipients of their pastoral care. This has resulted in passivity among the people of God. The role of pastors has come to be responders rather than proactive strategic thinkers and equippers. Here the members are the spectators, and the clergy is at center stage. The members are expected to do three simple things: show up, pay up, and shut up.

The missional church is more organic than institutional.

This quickly leads to the consumer mind-set where the members critique and evaluate the "return for the investment" and decide whether they will stay. As a result, pastors become stressed trying to keep the members happy. The mission of Jesus is somewhere on the back burner. Robert Lewis describes this kind of church like this: "The church functioning as a refuge from the world becomes sort of a Christian club that exhausts itself trying to keep its members happy."[3]

[3] Robert Lewis, *The Church of Irresistible Influence* (Grand Rapids: Zondervan, 2001), 9.

The missional church is more organic than institutional. The clergy is not center stage, and neither are the members. Jesus is the central focus. Why? Because it is *His* church! He is the head. His mission is the believer's mandate.

In the organic church, everyone is a priest—a minister, a missionary. It is recognized that God has a calling on each believer's life and that baptism is a sending forth. Every Christ-follower is called and gifted to join the mission of God on the earth, once they are properly equipped.

Transition from the institutional to organic will require a shift to an equipping model. This model is clearly the New Testament paradigm for church leadership. Paul, in Ephesians, sets forth the job description and function of church leadership.

> *And He Himself gave some to be apostles, some prophets, some evangelists, and some pastors and teachers, for the equipping of the saints for the work of ministry, for the edifying of the body of Christ* (Ephesians 4:11, 12).

When Jesus ascended back to the Father, He gave the church strategic servant-leaders (apostles, prophets, evangelists, and pastor-teachers). Their purpose was clear: *prepare God's people for works of service (ministry).*

The graphic below may help to visualize this principle more clearly.

It is evident from this passage that the overarching role of the servant-leaders of the church is not to "do the work of the ministry" but to "equip God's people for the work of the ministry." Quaker Theologian Elton Trueblood said

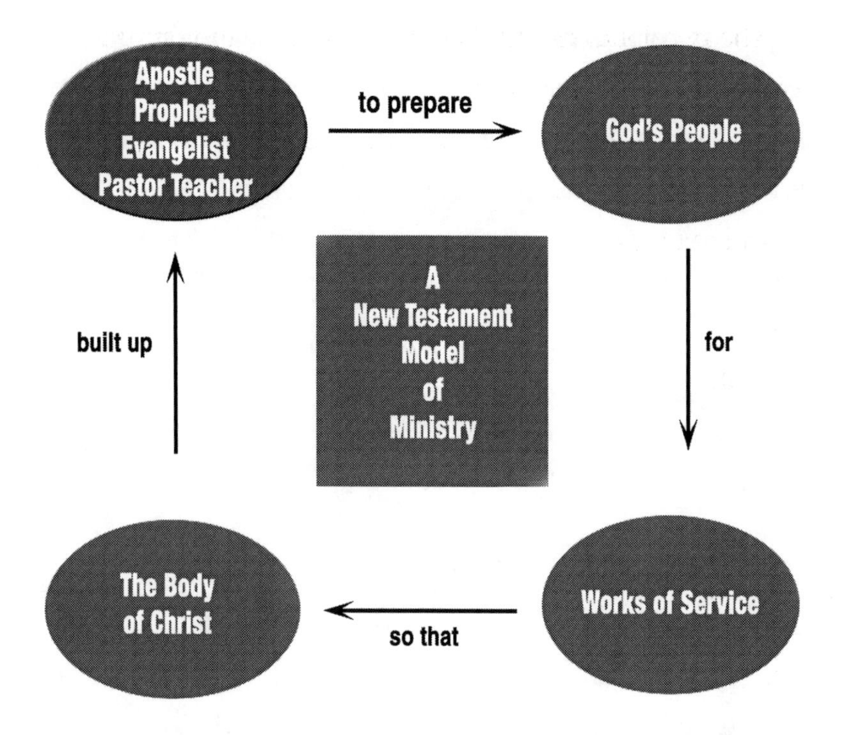

it well. "The ministry is for all who are called to share in Christ's life. The pastorate is for those who possess the peculiar gift of being able to help other men and women practice any ministry to which they have been called."[4] Essentially, the church leaders' first priority is to so invest themselves in other individuals that they will become missionaries of Jesus Christ. It is to give oneself in such a way as to bring the ministry of all God's people to functioning practical reality.

Discovering Spiritual Gifts

One of the essentials of the equipping model is helping believers understand their giftedness. A maximum of fruitfulness and fulfillment happens when individuals serve in

4 David Elton Trueblood, *The Incendiary Fellowship* (New York: Harper & Row, 1978), 33.

ways that correspond to their giftedness. Therefore, equipping people for the ministry and mission of Jesus must include opportunities for Christ-followers to understand the theology of spiritual gifts and to discover and deploy their gifts in serving.

Every believer is strategically placed in the body of Christ and given a special ability (a spiritual gift) by the Holy Spirit that enables him or her to serve the purpose of God.

The theology of spiritual gifts is quite simple: Every believer is strategically placed in the body of Christ and given a special ability (a spiritual gift) by the Holy Spirit that enables him or her to serve the purpose of God. Peter wrote, "As each one has received a gift, minister it to one another, as good stewards of the manifold grace of God" (1 Peter 4:10). Three key words related to spiritual gifts spring from this passage:

- *Each*: No believer is overlooked. Every follower of Christ has received a spiritual gift.
- *Minister*: Gifts are not for identification purposes, but for serving. Believers' gifts should be their pathway to serving, defining their mission or purpose in life.
- *Grace*: Spiritual gifts furnish the way the grace of God most naturally flows through a believer's life. Spiritual gifts are the conduits of the grace of God to others.

Paul says that there are three categories of spiritual gifts in 1 Corinthians 12:4-7. A balanced doctrine of spiritual gifts requires that believers understand the subtle differences between these different groups of gifts. Paul wrote:

> *There are* different kinds of gifts, *but the same Spirit. There are* different kinds of service, *but the same Lord. There are* different kinds of working, *but the same God works all of them in all men. Now to each one the manifestation of the Spirit is given for the common good (NIV, italics mine).*

The phrase "different kinds" occurs three times in this passage, indicating that Paul is referencing three groupings of spiritual gifts. The diversity of the gifts is balanced by the unity of the Godhead who is the source of the gifts, as indicated by the word "same" that is found three times in the text. Whatever the gift, when it is in operation, it is not the manifestation of human ability or ingenuity. It is a manifestation of the Spirit.

Manifestation Gifts

The "manifestation gifts" are most likely the nine gifts that Paul immediately lists in the next three verses in 1 Corinthians 12:

> *To one is given the word of wisdom through the Spirit, to another the word of knowledge through the same Spirit, to another faith by the same Spirit, to another gifts of healings by the same Spirit, to another the working of miracles, to another prophecy, to another discerning of spirits, to another different kinds of tongues, to another the interpretation of tongues* (1 Corinthians 12:8-10).

These gifts should not be considered permanent endowments of any believer but as gifts that may be manifested through any yielded Christian as the Holy Spirit determines. Hence, they are given the designation "various kinds of working." The Greek word is *energéma* from which comes the English word "energy." These gifts demonstrate the power and energy of the Holy Spirit working uniquely through and among His people to bring attention to the gospel, to affirm God's presence among His people, to comfort, encourage, and exhort, to heal and to guide, and to be a sign of God's Kingdom.

One might think of the manifestation of these gifts as "the dancing hand of God."

Probing the word "manifestation," its roots come from two Latin words. *Mani* has to do with the hand, and *fest* means "fiesta, feast, or dance." One might think of the manifestation of these gifts as "the dancing hand of God." When the congregation gathers, the hand of God "dances" over the congregation and comes to rest upon a particular member, who is used of the Spirit to manifest a gift.

Ministry Gifts

The "ministry gifts" are most likely the gifts found in Ephesians 4:7-8; 11-12:

> But to each one of us grace was given according to the measure of Christ's gift. Therefore He says:

When He ascended on high,
He led captivity captive,
And gave gifts to men."

> And He Himself gave some to be apostles, some prophets, some evangelists, and some pastors and teachers, for the equipping of the saints for the work of ministry, for the edifying of the body of Christ.

The Greek word for service is *diakonia,* from which our English word "deacon" is derived. It typically refers to one who ministers under the command or orders of another. The ministry gifts are gifts of people who are uniquely qualified to serve under the lordship of Christ. As referenced earlier, these are servant-leaders who are distinctively called to serve the body in such a way that the people of God are equipped for the work of the ministry so that the church is strengthened in the mission of God.

The ministry gifts are gifts of people who are uniquely qualified to serve under the lordship of Christ.

Motivational Gifts

The third gift group is the motivational gifts. These gifts are found in Romans 12:4-8:

> Just as each of us has one body with many members, and these members do not all have the same function, so in Christ we who are many form one body, and each member belongs to all the others. We have different gifts, according to the grace given us. If a man's gift is *prophesying,* let him use it in proportion to his faith. If it is *serving,* let him serve; if it is *teaching,*

> let him teach; if it is *encouraging*, let him encourage; if it is *contributing* to the needs of others, let him give generously; if it is *leadership*, let him govern diligently; if it is *showing mercy*, let him do it cheerfully (*NIV*, italics mine).

With regard to the equipping paradigm, this list of gifts is the most significant gift category. Unlike the manifestation gifts, which are spontaneous incidences of the Holy Spirit's working among believers, the motivational gifts are permanent endowments. Every believer has been given one or more of these gifts (note the phrase: "we *have* different gifts"), and this gifting is part of the matrix that determines fruitful and fulfilling ministry.

Another way of looking at the motivational gifts is to see them as the believer's priestly ministry. This is where serving is offered as worship to God. At the beginning of Romans 12, Paul introduces his discourse on these gifts with a strong allusion to this.

> *I urge you, brothers, in view of God's mercy, to offer your bodies as living sacrifices, holy and pleasing to God—this is your spiritual act of worship. Do not conform any longer to the pattern of this world, but be transformed by the renewing of your mind. Then you will be able to test and approve what God's will is—his good, pleasing and perfect will. For by the grace given me I say to every one of you: Do not think of yourself more highly than you ought, but rather think of yourself with sober judgment, in accordance with the measure of faith God has given you* (Romans 12:1-3, *NIV*).

The priesthood theme of this passage is often overlooked, but it is obvious that it was in Paul's mind as he wrote. First, the reference to believers giving their bodies as living sacrifices brings up the image of the Old Testament priests who administered the sacrificial system of Jewish law. Then, Paul's use of the Greek word *latreia* for worship (*service* in some translations) also continues this priesthood motif. It is a term that was used to describe a priest in complete self-surrender performing his duties before God. Clearly, then, the motivational gifts are the gifts of priesthood. They are the means by which God's people live out in practical ways the doctrine of the priesthood of every believer, thus fulfilling the overall mission of the church.

The following graphic helps illustrate the flow of Romans 12:

The following chart is an overview of the motivational gifts that will help in defining some of the essential characteristics of these gifts:

	Prophesying	Serving	Teaching	Encouraging	Giving	Ruling	Showing Mercy
Description	Readily perceives the will of God and labors for its accomplishment	Quickly sees the practical needs of the work of God and desires to help meet them	Searches out truth and presents it in ways that lead to understanding	Helps others to see the practical application of truth to life and stimulates their faith	Desires to use material possessions to bless people and the work of God	Has the ability to coordinate the activities of others to achieve God-honoring goals	Easily perceives the distress of others and responds with compassion
Characteristics	Assertive/bold A "big picture" person Sees things as black and white	Unselfish Works behind the scenes Stays until the job is done	Studious Systematic Accuracy is important	Coach/Mentor Patient with others Empathetic	Gives anonymously Sensitive to financial needs Manages well	Organizer Visionary Enjoys working with people	Empathetic Kind and loving Inner strength and optimism
Potential Strengths	Can stand alone Concerned with righteousness Uncompromising	Sees what needs to be done Energetic	Objective Presents truth in clear manner Factual	Positive and optimistic Persuasive Simplifies complex issues	Very generous Careful to give wisely Practices good stewardship	Inspires confidence of others Uses resources wisely Persevering	Protective of the weak Peacemaker Spontaneously tenderhearted
Potential Weaknesses	Can be critical and legalistic Can be harsh and insensitive Can feel superior	Can have difficulty saying 'no' Can be easily frustrated	Can see knowledge as an end not a means to an end Can be impatient with those who disagree	Can focus on 'feel good' solutions rather than real solutions Can use scripture out of context	Can easily be taken advantage of Can focus on more temporal values rather than eternal values	Can be opportunistic Can 'use' people Can be egotistical	Can be oversensitive and easily hurt Can be meddlesome and intrusive Can be indecisive
Biblical Example	Peter John, the Baptist	Andrew Timothy Martha	Luke Apollos The Bereans	Paul	Barnabas The Macedonians	Nehemiah James, the brother of Jesus	John, the Apostle

The Gift Discovery Process

A gift discovery process will involve three key elements. First, there is the *vision-casting phase.* This phase begins with dialoging and sharing the vision of transitioning the church to an equipping model with the leaders of the church. Conversations and times of prayer are essential catalytic moments that are crucial to the reshaping of a church. All leaders should do their homework and share their hearts with the team. Also, they should share the resources and materials that have been a part of forming their thoughts on this matter. Cover all this in prayer, believing that a commitment to the vision will be forged by the Holy Spirit. Do not take a shortcut. This will take time, but it will be time well spent. This may take weeks or months. It took our leadership team almost two years to develop the mission statement for Metro Church.

Conversations and times of prayer are essential catalytic moments that are crucial to the reshaping of a church.

The second phase is the *teaching phase*. These should be messages and lessons designed to create hunger in the hearts of the people to help them see the clear teaching of Scripture. Messages preached from the pulpit can be reinforced with small group and Sunday School materials where sermon content can be discussed further and digested.

The final phase is the *discovery phase*. In this phase, the leaders call for a pilot group of people who would like to enter the journey of discovering their spiritual gifts. An orientation event helps the group understand the important connection between gift discovery and personal ministry. The use of a spiritual gifts analysis tool is usually a highlight of the event. People really get excited about getting a handle on what God has deposited in their lives. (A gifts analysis is included in the appendix and further discussed on the Web site accompanying this book, *www.greatcommission.cc*).

Identifying Passion

Leaders of equipping churches also recognize the importance of spiritual passion. Passion can be thought of as one's "heart." It is a burden that one is willing to bear with joy. It's like a calling that cannot be shaken. For Paul, it was the passion of the Gentiles. For Moses, it was the emerging nation of Israel. In modern times, one can could consider Billy Graham, whose passion is evangelism; James Dobson, whose passion is the family; Mother Teresa, whose passion was the suffering people of Calcutta and the world; John Maxwell, whose passion is leadership; Ravi Zacharias, whose passion is apologetics; Ron Luce, whose passion is America's youth; Leonard Sweet, whose passion is the emerging church in a changing culture; or Larry Jones, whose passion is the poor and hungry children of America.

Like spiritual gifts, passion is also God-given and Spirit-awakened.

Like spiritual gifts, passion is also God-given and Spirit-awakened. Five descriptive terms seem to best describe the ministry of the church as it is portrayed in the New Testament: Sanctuary, Army, Hospital, Family, and School. A balanced church will function well in each of these arenas because God will place a passion for each of these.

1. **The Sanctuary.** There are those who are passionate about the sanctuary or holy place of God. Worship leaders are sanctuary people. They are passionate about leading people

into the presence of God. They can and do spend much time in prayer and planning of worship experiences. They pull together other people with a similar passion to form worship teams and "armies of praise." While every Christ-follower is a worshiper, there are those with a "worship passion," and they help the others to worship.

2. **The Army.** People with this passion are "kingdom advancers." These are the Rambos of the body of Christ. They are keenly aware of and willing to engage the kingdom of darkness. They want to plant new churches, engage in spiritual warfare, and present the gospel to the lost. They are ready to take it to the street. They often unnerve people who do not share their passion, but that's all right. They are the spiritually militant arm of the church who recognize that the battle is not against flesh and blood, but against spiritual forces of darkness (Ephesians 6:10, 11). They live by Matthew 11:12, "The kingdom of heaven has been forcefully advancing, and forceful men lay hold of it" (*NIV*).

3. **The Hospital.** These people are passionate about ministering to hurting people, broken marriages, abused kids, people addicted to alcohol. These are the nurturers, the caregivers, the counselors of the church. They want to help broken people get put back together. Part of the mission of God is to heal the brokenhearted (Luke 4:18, 19). Often the army people rescue the broken and bring them to the hospital people. Army people aren't into fixing—they are into capturing and rescuing, saying, "We found them. We got them in. Can you fix them up?" Hospital people are passionate about helping broken people get fixed up.

4. **The Family.** The family people are the ones who are concerned about the meeting place—the "house." They are the people who say: "You know, we have got to keep this place looking nice. Somebody's got to cut the grass. Somebody's got to clean this place up. Somebody's got to welcome guests when they come. Somebody's got to teach and care for the children. Somebody's got to care about grandma and grandpa. Somebody's got to help the single moms. Somebody needs to plan the fellowship dinner and set it up." They step right in and see that these things happen. Why? Because the household—the family—is their passion.

5. **The School.** School people want to teach and explain. They are presenters. They are concerned about the biblical literacy of the people of God. They have no problem spending hours in prayerful study and preparation. They are challenged by the warning of Hosea, "My people are destroyed for lack of knowledge" (Hosea 4:6).

In the way God has designed the church, everyone doesn't do everything. Everyone does something.

How does one recognize his passion? Passion is what will cause an individual to engage in conversation until late in the night. One's passion is what he will spend money on. It is what causes him to register for a conference. One's passion is what he wants to get better at.

The church leaders' equipping plan should help people discern where their spiritual passion is and to help them develop it. There is a spiritual passion analysis included in the appendix that may help with this process.

The Servant Profile

Each believer has a "servant profile." It is the unique blend of one's spiritual gifts, which answers the question "How will I serve?" and one's spiritual passion, which answers the question, "Where should I serve?" So now comes the most important question, "Now what?"

Prior to the teaching event, the church should have identified all the present ministry/serving opportunities and related them to one of the five functions of the church. For instance, an adult Sunday school class would more than likely be a function of the school. The benevolence ministry would relate to the hospital. Intercessory prayer would probably be an army ministry. The praise team is clearly about the sanctuary. And, the greeter is about the family.

The aim is that "sweet spot" where giftedness, passion and spiritual maturity overlap.

Now church leaders are ready to move to the next step of equipping—the one-on-one interview. Here, the participants have a conversation with one of the church leaders who helps them understand their servant profile and discusses with them what ministry areas they are most likely to enjoy and feel fruitful and fulfilled in doing. The aim is that "sweet spot" where giftedness, passion and spiritual maturity overlap.

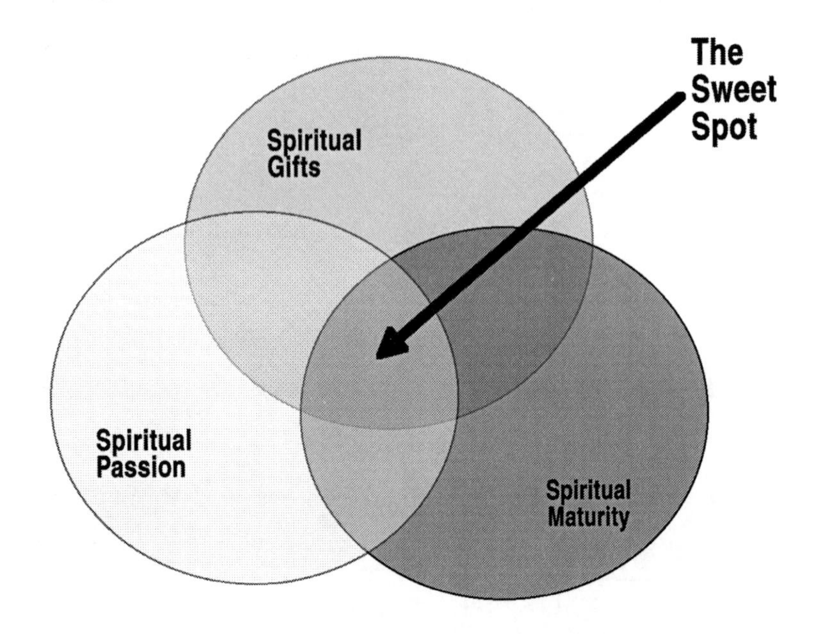

Don't be surprised if in this process of connecting spiritual gifts with spiritual passion that new ministries are born! When the clergy-dependent model begins to diminish, the people of God will step forward. God told Pharaoh to "Let my people go." He says the same to the church. It has yet to be seen what creative and spiritually vibrant ministries develop when the priesthood of the believer is fully implemented!

Letting the Spirit Lead

When we were about three years into the process of our church in Birmingham, I became frustrated by having begun many programs without seeing many lasting results. I came to a crisis point when one of the women of the church said to me, "Why don't we ever finish anything we start? Every time we start a new ministry, the fire seems to go out of the ministry we were engaged in before. When I look at our church, I see little piles of ashes where all these ministries have stopped."

After being stunned by these words, and at first being somewhat defensive, I agreed with her. I looked over the landscape of our first three years and saw it strewn with the debris of programs and ministries.

During a time of prayer for a period of months, I sensed the Holy Spirit saying to me, "Don't begin another program, ever!"

I argued within myself: "If I don't, nothing will happen."

Then He helped me to realize that He is lord of the church; He will create what is needed. I was to equip the people by preaching and teaching about serving in the Kingdom and by challenging them with opportunities. Every gift that is needed, He had already given. Let Him develop them.

Out of desperation, I finally said yes to the Lord's direction. After about six months, everything died. One day a leader in the church remarked to me, "Nothing's going on in our church! It would be exciting if we would just have a fight!"

Things rocked on for several weeks. Slowly but surely, people began to step forward and say they were called to start certain ministries. It was one of the turning points in the life of the church, and it was one of the crisis points of my personal ministry. Out of it I learned that it is His church and He will guide it if I will step back and let him.

Continued training, support, and coaching are a part of the equipping model. Remember, these ministers are not paid in the traditional sense. Money is not the motivation, but they do need to get "paid" with encouraging words, affirmation, clear directions, resources, gratitude, and empowerment. Watch them grow and applaud the fruit of their efforts. An equipping leader takes delight in highlighting and shining the spotlight on the ministry of others. There is no greater pleasure than believing in and seeing the ministry of others radiate. Let Christians shine!

Jesus told his disciples, "The harvest truly is plentiful, but the laborers are few" (Matthew 9:37). The harvest is not measured by the grain gathered in the barn, but by the wheat still standing in the field. As long as the church continues to operate with a clergy-dependent paradigm, the harvest will continue to go unreaped. Someone has said that Christianity in America is a lot like a professional football game. There are 22 people on the field who desperately need some rest, and 50,000 in the stands who desperately need some exercise.

When members of the body of Christ know they are genuine ministers, called by Jesus to the mission of God, something significant happens. When the saints are affirmed, equipped, and empowered to do the work of the ministry, the harvest will be reaped. That's the promise of Jesus!

The Last Word

Being properly equipped for ministry before launching into it is vitally important.

Living in Northern California some years ago, I came to love hiking and backpacking. On a warm June day, I started with four friends into the Desolation Wilderness on the

Nevada border. Our goal was Pyramid Peak, a nearly 10,000 foot climb in the Crystal Range. We planned a three-day trip, camping along the way.

The weather was beautiful, with azure blue skies and crystal clear vistas. As we reached the higher elevations, however, we saw snow still 10 feet deep. I have a fair complexion, and soon the combination of bright sunlight and glaring snow began to have its effect. Unfortunately, when I had filled my backpack with food and other necessities, I had neglected to include sun block. By the second morning, I needed it badly.

Disciples of Christ are ready for service when they are equipped, when they have unwrapped their gifts, when they have identified their passion, and when they have found the place where they fit in Kingdom service.

While we were preparing breakfast around the campfire, one of the group observed that the principal ingredient in sun block is oil; why not use bacon grease to serve the same purpose? It sounded reasonable to me, so I liberally smeared it all over my face. As a matter of fact, however, it didn't block anything. It multiplied the strength of the sunlight.

By the time we reached home, my face was covered with huge blisters. The doctor who treated me told me I had second-degree burns, and I was in danger of severe scarring. It was a long and painful recovery, and it taught me important lessons.

Good intentions are not enough. Lacking proper equipment can cause catastrophe. How many people have failed because they have the wrong equipment? How many are blistered and broken because they started off ill-equipped?

Disciples of Christ are ready for service when they are equipped, when they have unwrapped their gifts, when they have identified their passion, and when they have found the place where they fit in Kingdom service.

Equipping Points

1. Equipping means providing specific equipment for discovering, developing and deploying individual spiritual gifts, callings, and assignments.
2. Be clear about doctrinal truths and devotional requirements. Leaders cannot give more than they have and can't lead farther than they've been.
3. Keep the equipping process spiritual through prayer with those with whom you are working and by laying on hands and anointing.
4. Give people permission to experiment with their gifts to find a mission fit.
5. Keep *mission*—not *ministry*—before those you equip, because you will equip both people who will serve the church and those who will serve the community. Mission keeps the big picture before the people. It raises the bar from "church work" to "the mission of the church."
6. Study the various gifts and callings in order to be prepared to answer questions.
7. Do not be afraid to admit "I don't know," if you don't know. Ask the group, "What do you think?"
8. Do not set expectations too high. Everyone does not wish to be equipped.
9. Keep the big mission picture before people as "larger than life, making life meaningful, asking people to give their life away, the call of God for everyone."
10. Make equipping a big deal and stay enthusiastic at every training session.
11. Equip at a time when people can easily participate, e.g., Sunday evening and Wednesday night.
12. Set equipping sessions at four to six weeks. People tire if they have to invest too much time.
13. Let people hear from leaders who are "on the field," ministering in missional areas, e.g., Sunday school workers, ushers, street evangelism, food distribution, prayer-walking.

Chapter 6

Empowering— The Dynamic of the Commission

"But you shall receive power when the Holy Spirit has come upon you; and you shall be witnesses to Me in Jerusalem, and in all Judea and Samaria, and to the end of the earth" (Acts 1:8).

When my dad started preaching, he did not own a car, but he felt it necessary to buy one, paying the monthly payments from the offerings that came in the revivals he was preaching. Sometimes the offerings were inadequate, however, so eventually he got behind in the car payments. Dad told his grandfather, John C. Padgett, one of the Church of God's pioneer preachers, "I'm behind in my car payments. I've arranged to get a job so I can catch up these payments."

Without blinking, Granddad Padgett responded, "Make car payments? Listen, I have had to feed and clothe my wife, nine children and me. I have walked on the railroad track regularly nine miles one way to go and preach three times. The soles of my shoes have worn out, so that I have stuffed cardboard in my shoes to be able to keep going. I've done all this without a car. But you're going to stop preaching so you can drive a car? Have you been called to preach or to ride in a car?"

Dad never took the job. He kept preaching, and God honored his commitment. God honors that kind of commitment today from men and women who want to be equipped and empowered to serve in His harvest.

Empowerment takes two forms: first, it requires an understanding of God's calling and the world to which believers are called; second, it requires the anointing of the Holy Spirit.

This chapter explores the need for believers today to be empowered to share their faith with a spiritually needy world. Empowerment takes two forms: first, it requires an understanding of God's calling and the world to which believers are called; second, it requires the anointing of the Holy Spirit.

God's Calling

First, a statement of truth: the Great Commission will never be accomplished without the laity of the church. Plain and simple. The people of God are the workers God has chosen to partner with Him in the fulfillment of this exciting command to the body of Christ. The traditional church view regarding the laity—one that has been heard for years—is, "Every believer a minister."

Reggie McNeal, in a thought-provoking book,[1] challenges this assumption. He says, "Every time I see the slogan 'Every member a minister' I cringe. It usually means that there has been a lot of effort put into getting church members to get church work done." McNeal calls this "myopic vision" and says it has resulted in ministry being defined largely in church terms and lay people often being viewed as functionary resources to get church work done.

For many years, I used this terminology, "Every member a minister," but the phrase intentionally and subtly limits the concept of ministry to a setting within the local church. I have come to think in different terms: Every member is a *missionary.*

If Evelyn, a nurse by vocation, goes on a short-term missions trip to Guatemala, she is called a medical missionary. It is my contention that when she goes to work at the hospital in Kansas City, or wherever she lives, she's a missionary there, too.

The work of the church is not always in the church—it is *Kingdom* work. The ministry of the laity goes far beyond the four walls of local congregations. Laity need more than just "jobs in the church." They have been called and gifted by

1 Reggie McNeal, *The Present Future* (San Francisco: Jossey-Bass Publishers, 2009), 87.

our Lord for ministry in the community as well. The Great Commission doesn't say, "Go into all the *church* and make *workers* of all nations, *nagging* them in the name of the Lord."

An easy-to-remember definition of ministry is that it is Christian work that involves the acts, duties, and services of all believers where they live, work, and worship. Ministry is any human activity that is entered into on behalf of Jesus and His gospel. The word "minister" is not only a noun, but also a verb. Ministry involves identifying and meeting human needs spiritually, socially, and physically. Believers move beyond "talk" and actually "do." The extra dimension the word *missionary* gives to ministry is the connotation that the ministry takes place in a setting to which a person is *sent,* and it often signifies a ministry to a different culture. When the missionary goes to another country, it is defined by cultural differences in terms of geography and language; however, there are more subtle implications of cultural distinction. It's possible in today's world for the family across the street to belong to a different culture.

Christian Calling

The church has wrestled long, but never definitively, with the problem of Christian vocation and daily work in the secular world. Are laymen and women "called," or are only clergymen? Can daily work in the secular world be or ever become "sacred?" A better understanding of the term "vocation" might be helpful. It comes from the Latin *vocatio* which means "to summon" or "to call." Vocation was originally used in the 15th century for the call into the priesthood or a religious order. Only those in religious work had a vocation or calling—everyone else simply had a job to make a living. Gradually, vocation came to be broadened to include all people and came to mean the work in which a person is regularly employed. The truth is that all of life, including one's job, or employment is a calling from God.

The church has wrestled long, but never definitively, with the problem of Christian vocation and daily work in the secular world.

The success of the fulfillment of the Great Commission really hinges on the laity understanding the call and responding to it.[2] The invitation is really a life calling or general call from God to all people to live a life of service. Every Christian has a life calling from God. A life calling answers one of the deepest questions of life—Why am I here? A life calling is different from career planning, or even vocational choice—it is about what believers need to do with their lives to accomplish God's great plan on earth. Their role in cooperating with God to bring this to pass becomes their life calling. A life calling will influence one's vocational choices, but it is much bigger than a person's career or job. Finding one's life calling may be the most important thing a believer can do, for it is discovering his/her purpose for living. It is what God wants His people to do with their lives.

2 I have dealt extensively with the issue of calling in my book, *No Church Left Behind* (Cleveland, Tenn.: Pathway Press) See p. 158 ff.

Primary among Christians' purposes in daily life, where they work and reside, must be the conviction that believers are placed in this world, and in a particular spot in the world, as "salt" and "light" (Matthew 5:13-16). When Jesus described Christians as salt and light, He was not speaking about just the *possibility* of being salt and light. He made a bold statement and said believers *are* salt and light, and not only that, they are *all* the salt and light the world has. Wherever God's people are, however penetrating their light, they are all of it there is. In their communities, in their workplaces, in their recreation settings—salt and light will be coming from Christ-followers who believe that they can make a difference in the lives of others around them.

He made a bold statement and said believers are salt and light, and not only that, they are all the salt and light the world has.

The best way to do this is by developing one-to-one relationships with unbelievers and the unchurched. One-to-one personal witnessing requires transparency and living the Christlike life every day. There is no room for any holier-than-thou attitude.

Missionaries at Home

Churches should not want to move away from the laity becoming ministers, but the laity must also learn to think like *missionaries*. God is looking for lay men and women who will accept the call to become a "minister," get involved in "ministry," and then learn the wisdom of the mind of a "missionary."

When missionaries go to a foreign culture, they must (1) learn all about the culture, (2) respect the culture, (3) communicate to the culture, and (4) reach the lost within the culture with the message of salvation. The current term for all of this is "missiology." The technical meaning of this term is "mission science" and is defined as the area of practical theology which investigates the mandate, message, and work of the Christian missionary.

There are 168 hours in a week and believers must be accountable for all of them.

If believers are to win the world, beginning at home, they must become culturally relevant missionaries in their thinking and approach. The believer's culture is not the world's culture; the Christian's beliefs are not the world's beliefs. Believers must understand the culture so they can build bridges to it for the sake of gaining a hearing for the gospel of Jesus.

Brian McLaren, pastor of Cedar Ridge Community Church, Washington, D.C., says that the church has to approach the culture with a missionary strategy as though it were presenting the gospel for the first time.[3] Christian faith thrives in this kind of situation and provides believers with wonderful ministry opportunities.

---

3 This is a recurring theme in McLaren's books, including *A New Kind of Christian, The Story We Find Ourselves In*, and *A Generous Orthodoxy*.

Elton Trueblood, the Quaker theologian, called it our "Other Vocation." It has to do with the investment of one's gifts in addition to daily work and community life. To be on duty for Christ in the world of work involves more than just a 40-hour work week. There are 168 hours in a week and believers must be accountable for all of them. Their role is to step out in faith, learn about the culture, start conversations, ask questions, explore all of the open doors, and leave the rest up to God.

New or Old?

The timeless message of the Great Commission always has to be considered in the context of the world as it exists today. We are told that our world is a "postmodern world." What does this really mean to the Evangelical church? I remember years ago, before the Oldsmobile division of General Motors ceased production, they came out with a commercial featuring the words, "This is not your father's Oldsmobile." The implication, of course, was that it was a new and modern vehicle and that it had undergone great changes. This is a verbal image of our world as we know it today—it has undergone great change. One of the current buzzwords is *raplexity*, which is defined as "rapid and complex change." Society has moved from a modern world to a postmodern world.

This is the age of the experiential and visual. In this age, everyone is connected and is told there are few (if any) absolutes. In just one generation, history moved from a "Gutenberg world" to a "Google world." The printed page is being replaced by the electronic page of e-mails, text messages, and the Internet. Just to stay in touch, people must have a Facebook page and be signed up to Twitter.

Called to the Culture

Who are the people populating the postmodern nation? They are not just the pierced and tattooed. This group includes just about everybody under the age of 40. They have been described in different terms—postmodern, Gen-X, even the overused "contemporary." They have always had a PIN number; they have grown up with computers as a way of life. There has never been a time when they have not had a cell phone. They are parents as well as kids; they are teachers as well as students. They are engineers as well as artists. They make up the community. They are neighbors. They are the future church.

They seem to be information rich, but upon close examination, they are spiritually poor. They believe that there are many ways to God. They need the spiritual wisdom that only God can give them. The challenge is to help change their minds about pluralistic thinking. How do Christians reach postmoderns who believe, "It's fine for you, but not for me"?

This new era of postmodernism officially began in 1960, but as with all historical transitions, it has taken some time to show up in daily life. Universities are generally one of the first places where new ideas take hold, while culture at large lags behind. And what lags behind in the general culture is usually true of the Christian culture.

One well-known church consultant had this to say after visiting many churches that were literally in a time warp and still trying to do God's business with traditional methods. He said, "Well, if 1957 ever comes back, I personally know of many congregations that will be ready for it!"[4] How do Christians reach this new culture? One thing is for sure: they can't go backwards in time. L. P. Hartley said it this way: "The past is a foreign country; they do things differently there."[5]

Facing Culture

When it comes to culture, Christians generally have one of three attitudes: fight it, join it, or engage it.

1. **Fight it**. The church hears generalizations like "Everything in this culture is wrong." Ironically, when the world was heavily in the era of modernism, few churches bought into it wholeheartedly. But now that history is past modernism, many are longing for the good old days. Change is resisted, and the old ways are used—even if they are not working. The ministry of local churches is sometimes segmented from other parts of life (business, family, recreation, etc.), resulting in a disconnect between the church and the community.

This is a reality especially with two groups in the church: men and boys. Man in the Mirror Ministries, a parachurch group in Florida, says that 25 percent of women in church worship without their husbands, and 90 percent of the boys who are being raised in the church will abandon it by their 20th birthday.

---

[4] George Hunter, *Church for the Unchurched* (Nashville: Abingdon, 1996), 36.

[5] L.P. Hartley, *The Go-Betweens* (London: Hamish Hamilton, 1953), 1.

2. **Join it**. The church can become conformed to the cultural values that surround it. Such groups are called "cultural churches," because they endorse the culture and blend in with it to the extent that they surrender their core beliefs just to reach others. Churches like this care little for society, think little of missions, evangelism, or social issues that must be addressed by believers. Some "seeker-oriented churches" continually face the temptation to put a priority on so-called relevance over truth. In other words, some churches willingly "water down the truth" in an attempt to be relevant and conform to the culture.

3. **Engage it**. In John 17: 14-15, Jesus said, "I have given them Your word; and the world has hated them because they are not of the world, just as I am not of the world. I do not pray that You should take them out of the world, but that You should keep them from the evil one." This truth is unchanging: believers are *in* the world but are not *of* the world. What then does the church do with the culture? The same thing Jesus did: engage it!

Luke 5:29-32 tells a beautiful story about Jesus engaging the culture.

> *Then Levi gave Him a great feast in his own house. And there were a great number of tax collectors and others who sat down with them. And their scribes and the Pharisees complained against His disciples, saying, "Why do You eat and drink with tax collectors and sinners?" Jesus answered and said to them, "Those who are well have no need of a physician, but those who are sick. I have not come to call the righteous, but sinners, to repentance.*

The big surprise was that Jesus would show up for this party. He did because His desire was, still is, and always will be "to seek and save that which was lost" (Luke 19:10). Jesus gave Himself. Can His followers do any less? They have to offer Jesus to the people of the world today. Paul never argued that Christ could top the mystery religions and other ecstatic cults in terms of religious experience. He offered the truth—Jesus Christ and Him crucified. This was the power of God to which he wanted them exposed.

The big surprise was that Jesus would show up for this party.

Postmodernists will respond to the gospel. They are looking for authentic relationships that offer meaning and connectedness. They are spiritually hungry.

It has been well said that the church is the "local branch office" of God's kingdom. It is the working agency of the Kingdom. As such, it exists for a twofold purpose: (1) to demonstrate the Kingdom, and (2) to spread it through obedience to His commands. The job of individual believers is to join the church in accomplishing these two goals.

It has been well said that the church is the "local branch office" of God's kingdom.

Jesus often spoke using metaphors. He used images like salt, light, keys, water, and fire. Each of these items has something in common: each figure represents some kind of penetration. The purpose of salt is to *penetrate* the meat and preserve it; the function of light is to *penetrate* the darkness; keys *penetrate* the lock; water *penetrates* the hard crust of the earth; and fire continues to consume unless contained. These figures make the goal of the church very clear. In effect, they were used to lead up to the last recorded words of Jesus which were words of commission. He gave the Great Commission in Matthew 28:19, 20 and His very last words before the Ascension in Acts 1:8: "But you shall receive power when the Holy Spirit has come upon you; and you shall be witnesses to Me in Jerusalem, and in all Judea and Samaria, and to the end of the earth." There is no question about it—Christians are to spread the Kingdom!

But *how*?

Christians spread the Kingdom by personal witness and by proclamation of the good news in the power of the Spirit.

Holy Spirit Power

Regardless of our mastery of programs and techniques—neither of which I deprecate—I must emphasize that the source of the church's authority and power lies in the Holy Spirit.

The Acts of the Apostles has sometimes been called "The Acts of the Holy Spirit," because so much of the book is dedicated to the deeds of the Spirit in the life of individual believers and the church. A survey of His actions in Acts teaches the church today what might be expected when He empowers them, what I have called "Dynamics of Great Commission Leadership."

Ten Dynamics of Great Commission Leadership

- *Separating.* "As they ministered to the Lord and fasted, the Holy Spirit said, "Now separate to Me Barnabas and Saul for the work to which I have called them" (Acts 13:2). The Spirit acted in the same manner as Jesus had done when He called his disciples to separate from the crowd and spend time in a retreat with Him (Mark 6:30-32). His calling to Great Commission obedience involves a "setting apart." Today the Holy Spirit calls the church to identity and intimacy with Christ, urging solitude when the world presses in too much. He separates believers from lesser concerns and impels them into His service.
- *Serving.* The Holy Spirit inspires service. When the young church grew in number and troubles arose, the apostles were led to appoint deacons who would handle the daily operations of the church, serving their brethren (see Acts 6:1-8). The principal qualification for the office was being "full of the Holy Spirit." The Spirit-filled Christian will always serve with humility. "You know, from the first day that I came to Asia, in what manner I always lived among you, serving the Lord with all humility," Paul told the Ephesian elders (Acts 20:18, 19). The 21st-century church needs servant leaders, and the Holy Spirit will inspire them to service.

  The overarching rule for leadership is that spiritual leaders are first servants. They are not lords, not bosses, not celebrities, not dominators, not dictators, not manipulators, but servants. "You know that those who are considered rulers over the Gentiles lord it over them, and their great ones exercise authority over them. Yet it shall not be so among you; but whoever desires to become great among you shall be your servant" (Mark 10:42, 43). A person who is not willing to be a servant is not qualified to be a leader.

A person who is not willing to be a servant is not qualified to be a leader.

- *Seeing.* One of the promises of Pentecost is that "Your young men shall see visions" (Acts 2:17); and seeing opportunities, seeing possibilities, seeing results of faith were hallmarks of the Spirit-filled believers of Acts. The church is called by Jesus himself to "lift up your eyes and look at the fields, for they are already white for harvest" (John 4:35). The Holy Spirit today helps the church recognize the harvest and the possibility of reaping it.

  Vision for spiritual goals originates with God. For believers to perceive what God wishes to do, however, requires intentional sensitivity. They must be looking for His guidance. When someone asked Helen Keller what would be worse than being blind, she replied, "Having sight, but no vision."

  A third grade teacher instructed her students to perform an experiment at home. They were to go out into their backyards at night and count the stars. Their reports went all over the map: one student counted 125, another 210, and so forth; however, one little boy said he had counted only three stars. "How is that possible?" asked the teacher, to which the boy responded, "I have a really small backyard!" Vision requires intentionality.

- *Starting.* Again and again in the Book of Acts, the Holy Spirit is an initiator of action and ministry. He starts the church in Acts 2. He starts the service of deacons in Acts 6. He starts a revival in Samaria in Acts 8. He starts the ministry of Paul in Acts 9. Throughout the book, other examples are found of the originating. At the start of any new venture or ministry, it is vital to have measurable, meaningful, practical and directional roadmaps. Adjustments must be planned for, too, since nothing ever works out exactly as intended.
- *Strategizing.* "It seemed good to us, being assembled with one accord, to send chosen men to you with our beloved Barnabas and Paul" (Acts 15:25), shows that the Spirit led the church in making strategic decisions. The usual pattern seems to have been to permit Spirit-filled leaders to designate direction; then, if God wanted something different to ensue, the Spirit himself would interrupt the decision-making, as He did when He forbade Paul to preach in Asia and sent the vision of the man of Macedonia (see Acts 16) that took him to Europe instead. In today's world, where decision-making is vital, the Holy Spirit still guides.

- *Structuring.* The Holy Spirit is interested in the appropriate structure of the church, even in its details. Acts 1:26 clarifies how a new apostle was chosen to take the place of Judas. Titus 1:5 explains that Titus was sent by Paul to Crete to set the church in order. The Book of Acts in its entirety is the story of the connecting, converting, discipling, equipping, and empowering of the church by the power of the Holy Spirit.
- *Stretching.* The Holy Spirit continually opened the minds of the first-century Christians to new concepts, new ideas and new experiences. They had a monocultural expectation of the church's growth, until the Spirit revealed that He was calling Gentiles to faith as well as Jews. They seemed to think that apostolic leaders needed to serve tables, taking time away from prayer and ministry, until the Spirit taught them that others could participate in this kind of service. Numerous examples of His stretching the horizons of their thinking appear in the book. Believers today need the Spirit's stretching ministry to prevent dull and stolid thinking.

  Stretching also implies that believers will be tested with regard to loving people, particularly new converts. New converts do dumb things. (Don't we all?) They are new creations, many of whom have never heard, "I love you." They are often the products of broken lives. If Christ-followers do not have patience and love for them, who will?

- *Struggling.* "Since we have this ministry, as we have received mercy, we do not lose heart" (2 Corinthians 4:1), testified the apostle Paul. The early church leaders and missionaries faced various struggles, but in every situation they sensed the presence and comfort and strength of the Holy Spirit. Believers today face problems regarding their family, marriage, finances, and other difficulties. But resistance is a natural part of life; it is to be expected. Resistance creates opportunities for growth and development. By pushing against resistant forces, muscles are built up.

  Working in teams, as Paul almost always did, struggles can be overcome by a "forming, storming, norming, and performing" strategy. In "forming," team members get to know one another. In "storming," they explore alternative solutions. In "norming," they establish a way of working together, and in "performing" they enjoy solutions and victory.
- *Surrendering.* It is impossible for church leaders today to continually bear the burden of the church and its tasks without God's strength. The model for them is found in Paul's parting address to the Ephesians when he visited them for the final time. He said, "So now, brethren, I commend you to God and to the word of His grace, which is able to build you up and give you an inheritance among all those who are sanctified" (Acts 20:32). There is more than one kind of surrender necessary. Sometimes leaders must simply give up the need to be needed.

Sometimes leaders must simply give up the need to be needed.

- *Staying with it!* In one of his short stories, Irish writer Frank O'Connor describes the boyhood challenge he and his friends would face running across fields and orchards, coming to a wall that impeded progress. To climb it would be difficult, and to go around would take too long. He and his friends would simply toss their hats over the wall, leaving themselves no option but to climb over. Now they had no choice, they were committed, they *had* to get over the wall.

  In a *60 Minutes* television interview, a Sherpa guide from Mount Everest was asked about several of his tribesmen who had died on the mountain. "Would they have died if they had not been engaged in helping less-experienced climbers to the top?" the interviewer asked. "No, they would not have died," the Sherpa answered. "And what is so important about getting to the top of the mountain?" the host continued. After a pause, the mountain guide answered, "I can tell from your question that you have never been to the top."

  Any Christian who has been to the top of Mount Calvary knows its joy and victory, and realizes there is nothing like helping others get to the top.

  The Holy Spirit helps God-called and commissioned believers remain steadfast, obedient to their calling, until the work is done and Jesus returns.

Boxing In the Holy Spirit

The Holy Spirit has come to glorify Christ and to empower believers for ministry; however it is possible for today's Christians to "put the Spirit in a box," in a manner of speaking, that impedes His ability to perform His ministry among them. How is this done?

- *The "tongues" box.* The Holy Spirit announces His baptism in the life of a believer by a phenomenon called "speaking in tongues" (See Acts 2, 8, 9, 11, 19). This is a common occurrence that, although questioned and doubted by outsiders, has been experienced by multiplied millions around the globe since New Testament days and particularly in the last 100 years. The Spirit also employs tongues to pray through the experience of believers (Romans 8) and, in concert with a Spirit-inspired interpreter, to deliver prophetic truth to the church (1 Corinthians 14). But believers can box the Spirit in by limiting His work and witness to the phenomenon of tongues. His ministry is infinitely broader than this one aspect of His manifestation. The church should welcome the appearance of tongues, while recognizing that it is not the Spirit's most significant ministry.

The church should welcome the appearance of tongues, while recognizing that it is not the Spirit's most significant ministry.

- *The "temple" box.* Where does the Holy Spirit perform His ministry of anointing, equipping, empowering? The first response that comes to mind is "He does that in the church." Yes, He does. He gives gifts that may be employed in the context of a church service, He anoints the preacher standing behind the pulpit in the church building, He inspires singers to sing and teachers to teach, all in the church. But His ministry must not be limited, consciously or unconsciously, to the church. The scope of His work begins in church, but it moves beyond. Peter learned that God could move beyond, when God visited him on a rooftop near a seashore and told him to go to a distant city and open the Kingdom to non-Jewish believers (Acts 10, 11). Paul was inspired by the Spirit in the great cities of the Roman Empire, where no church as yet existed. When he arrived in Corinth, for instance, before any church had been initiated, the Spirit revealed to him that God already had many people in the city. The church today must not limit the Holy Spirit to what He can do within the church.
- *The "tradition" box.* How will the Holy Spirit manifest himself? Who will He empower and how will He go about it? The answers to those questions may be discerned to some extent by considering what He has done in the past. But is that all? Is tradition the church's only guide? No, the Spirit is imaginative and creative. In the Jewish setting of the first century when He came to fill the lives of believers, He was

first observed anointing male preachers; however, Peter captured His ultimate intent when he quoted Joel, "Your sons and daughters shall prophesy." Soon the Spirit had broken through the mold of "men only" preachers and had inspired women to preach also. At first it was anticipated that only Jewish people would be heirs of the Kingdom, but soon it became apparent that the Spirit's plans included Gentiles, too. The church must avoid limiting the Holy Spirit to what He has always done. Perhaps He wishes to do something new!

Soon the Spirit had broken through the mold of "men only" preachers and had inspired women to preach also.

- *The "time" box.* Everyone knows when the manifestation of the Spirit is expected to take place. It is likely it will happen between 10:30 a.m. and 12 noon on Sunday. Everyone knows that! It is possible, however, to structure a service in such a way that He does not sense the freedom to enter. When the Spirit does anoint a service, why do believers then leave the church and go out into the world for the other 166 hours of the week, to live among their family and friends and to go about their workaday world without any expectation that the Holy Spirit will do anything in their lives during that time? How foreign to the plan and desire of God! When a believer is filled with the Spirit, it is not a two-hours-per-week arrangement; it is a good 24 hours a day, seven days a week. Whether or not the Spirit is free to manifest His guiding and teaching and prompting and anointing and empowering all the time is completely up to the believers. The Spirit must not be placed in a time box.

Results of Holy Spirit Empowerment

Once believers are empowered by the Holy Spirit, what is the difference in their lives? They can claim the following benefits.

1. **Anointing.** God's anointing signifies a supernatural approval and guarantee of effectiveness (see 2 Corinthians 1:21 and 1 John 2:20). Just as Christ ("The Anointed One") was anointed by the Holy Spirit at His baptism, so believers today receive an anointing of the Spirit that increases the ease with which they announce God's good news.
2. **Calling.** When the New Testament speaks of a "calling," it generally refers to God's summons to people to become His children, His redeemed ones. In another sense, however, certain individuals are referred to as "called" to signify that they are set apart for God for particular ministry, e.g., Paul was called to be an apostle. The calling is a work of the Spirit.
3. **Authority.** "Encourage and rebuke with all authority" (Titus 1:5, *NIV*) was the charge given by Paul to Titus. Paul often claimed God-given authority to fulfill his ministry. Anyone who is called and commissioned

needs to sense that he is authorized for his work by the power of the Holy Spirit.

4. **Trust.** The epistles speak of the glorious gospel as a "trust" (1 Timothy 1:8) that was committed to certain individuals. Paul counseled Timothy to guard what was given to him in trust (1 Timothy 6:20). The Holy Spirit is the agent of God who entrusts a God-called man or woman with the treasure of the gospel. 1 Corinthians 9:17 uses the phrase "dispensation of the gospel committed to me" to affirm that individuals may be commissioned by Christ, through the Holy Spirit, to be responsible for ensuring that certain people receive the message of the gospel, and if they are not faithful to their calling, people will be lost as a result. It is a trust that God relies on His servants to fulfill.
5. **Overcoming power.** "You are of God, little children, and have overcome them, because He who is in you is greater than he who is in the world" (1 John 4:4) assures Christ-followers that the One (the Holy Spirit) who is in them is greater than the anti-Christ spirits that oppose them. Today's Spirit-filled believers are heir to the same promise.

From quite young, I sensed intuitively that I was called to preach. The confirmation came at a youth camp in Oregon in 1965 when I was almost 16 years old. Praying at the altar, I sensed God calling me. Shortly afterwards, a pastor invited me to preach in his church. For some reason, I didn't have the certainty of the calling and I told him I wasn't sure I was called. Soon, however, I accepted an invitation and went to the church. Several similar invitations came along, and I accepted them; but for the first few months, I didn't think of what I was doing as "preaching." I would give a talk. I felt no confidence, no authority behind what I was doing. Needless to say, it was not satisfying to me.

Questioning my calling, I finally spent a whole night in prayer in the garage of our home in Oregon—a cold December night. I asked God to either confirm the calling or remove it and let me know. I had felt empty when I was in the pulpit, and I was determined that I did not want to just deliver speeches. Toward the end of my praying, I sensed the Lord saying to me, "Raymond, it's not by might, nor by power, but by My Spirit. I am calling you and empowering you. Go, preach, and don't be afraid, for I am with you."

That's what I needed to hear. The next time I preached, in a little house church in Prineville, Oregon, I felt a liberty I had not experienced before. I preached with confidence and conviction from Ecclesiastes 12:1 "Remember now thy Creator in the days of thy youth" (KJV), to perhaps 30 people. That night an elderly man, in his `70s came and stood in front of me and said, "I don't remember what all you said tonight, but I want to give my heart to God!" He was the first convert under my preaching.

Empowerment means that someone trusts you and gives you authority and the confidence to go forward. God had done that for me. He will do that for all who put their trust in Him.

Empowering Points

1. Make sure those you empower pass the minimum "Three C's" test:
   Character—responsible, accountable, dependable, teachable
   Competence—loving, leading, listening to people
   Chemistry—shared ministry, vision, mission agreement with other leaders
2. Start small. You can't empower everbody, but you can empower somebody.
3. Invest time to listen, mentor, and coach individuals.
4. Stay in touch, using regular meetings and e-mail.
5. Celebrate successes and teach growth from failures.
6. Encourage.
7. Give space to people to take risks and fail.
8. Be secure. Let others shine, and give them credit.
9. Trust people.
10. Look for progress, not perfection.
11. Provide a budget, even if it is small.
12. Let missional leaders know, "It's your baby; you must rock it." Assure that decisions are made at the ministry level after consultation with those in authority.
13. Ask for regular reports from their area. This shows you care.
14. Catch people doing something good and make sure to compliment them.
15. Avoid, avoid, avoid micromanaging! You had to learn; let them learn, too.
16. Don't allow people to go around their leaders to get to you; ask, "Have you talked to your leader about this?"
17. Keep ministry decisions at the ministry level. Just require prior knowledge before decisions are inacted; tell leaders, "Don't surprise me."
18. Your security ensures that leaders trust you.
19. Know the four cycles of group development: Forming, storming, norming, performing.
20. Pray with and for your leaders.

21. Deal intentionally with problems and crises. Don't make one person's problem everyone's problem.
22. Provide in-service training for specific ministries at least once a year, using conferences, books, and DVDs.
23. Require Ministry Action Plans and state goals for the coming year. This specifies and provides clarity for leaders and followers.
24. Everyone empowered will not succeed. Some will fail, fall or just quit. How to respond? Adjust your flaps and keep flying.
25. Remember you are working with people, not robots. Be persevering, patient and exemplary. Someone is always watching you: Christ, church people, others.
26. It's impossible to empower beyond the level of your own empowerment. Pray much, read often, ask advice from those you trust, listen. You will hear what others have heard after a life of faithfulness: "Well done, good and faithful servant!"

Chapter 7

The Solution—
The Commitment to the Commission

This is a simple chapter. It aims to do four things.

If your church is not a Great Commission church, it lays out a proven change strategy that can help you get there.

1. If you are convinced that soulwinning in the local church is a priority, it describes a profoundly simply way to go about it.
2. If you have caught a vision for church planting and want ideas for how you can go about it, you will find suggestions.
3. If your vision for lost people who live outside North America has been clarified, I have identified ways you can move forward.

A Serious Error

Throughout this book, I have discussed what a Great Commission person (and a Great Commission church) is and does. One of the challenges Christians must face and overcome is the idea—prevalent in the thinking of many churches and denominations—that everything the church does is a Great Commission task. It *is* true that the local congregation's call to service is multifaceted, and ministry takes many forms.

John's version of the Great Commission includes the phrase, "As the Father sent me, so I send you." The personal ministry of Jesus himself was many-layered. He taught, He healed, He comforted, He fed the multitudes, and He worked other miracles for needy people. If today's Christ-followers are going to take His Word seriously, they will do a great deal more than preach, make disciples, baptize and teach. But no one should consider all those various kinds of ministries as fulfilling the Great Commission.

Believers must make their priority the winning of souls who will be incorporated into the Kingdom as disciples, and in turn, make other disciples.

The heart of one's ministry must be the Commission. Believers must make their priority the winning of souls who will be incorporated into the Kingdom as disciples, and in turn, make other disciples.

Paul does not quote the Great Commission, but his ministry breathes its essence. He writes to the Colossians, "All over the world this gospel is bearing fruit and growing, just as it has been doing among you since the day you heard it and understood God's grace in all its truth" *(1:6, NIV).* He was certain that the dynamic nature of the Word would guarantee its ongoing triumph and progress.

In 2 Corinthians 5:19, 20, he spells it out: "God was in Christ reconciling the world to Himself, not counting their trespasses against them, and He has committed to us the word of reconciliation. Therefore, we are ambassadors for Christ, as though God were making an appeal through us; we beg you on behalf of Christ, be reconciled to God" *(NASB).* I reiterate: Our primary task is helping people come to faith and assurance and folding them into the church as disciples.

Changing the Mind-set

If a church that is not presently a Great Commission church is to be changed, it is the task of the church leaders. This statement lays a heavy responsibility upon them, but it is one that comes with the territory.

I encourage church leaders to understand and assert spiritual authority in order to move the church in the direction of God's will. Some misunderstand spiritual authority and mislabel it as domination or subjugation. In God's way of doing things, it may be properly defined as "delegated influence from God through which He accomplishes His sovereign rule."

Luke 7:1-10 provides a useful case study for grasping the concept of spiritual authority.

> *Now when He concluded all His sayings in the hearing of the people, He entered Capernaum. And a certain centurion's servant, who was dear to him, was sick and ready to die. So when he heard about Jesus, he sent elders of the Jews to Him, pleading with Him to come and heal his servant. And when they came to Jesus, they begged Him earnestly, saying that the one for whom He should do this was deserving, "for he loves our nation, and has built us a synagogue." Then Jesus went with them. And when He was already not far from the house, the centurion sent friends to Him, saying to Him, "Lord, do not trouble Yourself, for I am not worthy that You should enter under my roof. Therefore I did not even think myself worthy to come to You. But say the word, and my servant will be healed. For I also am a man placed under authority, having soldiers under me. And I say to one, 'Go,' and he goes; and to another, 'Come,' and he comes; and to my servant, 'Do this,' and he does it." When Jesus heard these things, He marveled at him, and turned around and said to the crowd that followed Him, "I say to you, I have not found such great faith, not even in Israel!" And those who were sent, returning to the house, found the servant well who had been sick.*

The source of authority is crucial. The centurion in the story explains, "I am under authority." He was obeying someone who was over him and he was submissive to that leadership. Jesus, too, was under authority, the Father's authority. He willingly laid aside the independent assertion of His own power to do the will of the Father. The result was the fulfillment of God's will.

Any church leader who wants to move the church toward Great Commission obedience can do so in full authority of the Spirit.

Church leaders today operate under the authority of Christ and the Holy Spirit. Any church leader who wants to move the church toward Great Commission obedience can do so in full authority of the Spirit.

"Well, my problem is that most of the people in this church seem to believe that the church exists for their benefit. How am I going to get that to change?" I'm glad you asked.

Kotter's Process

In his book, *Leading Change*[1], John P. Kotter discusses the process of change. His guidelines, though taken from the business context, have been proven applicable to church life and the task of church leaders. He lists eight insights into the process of change.

1. ***Establish a sense of urgency.*** Take adequate time or this will be seen as just another "program" added to everything else. Looking at the state of society and the world today, considering the destination of those who are not Christ's disciples and expecting the return of Christ, the church is confronted with a biblically-inspired sense of urgency. It just needs to be preached and taught and hammered home to the congregation.

2. ***Create a guiding team.*** Not everyone in a church can be convinced to change their minds or their priorities at the same time. In most situations, however, insightful leaders can identify a small group of people from within the congregation who are influencers or who already evidence Great Commission commitment. Wise leaders will look for ways

[1] John Kotter, *Leading Change* (Boston: Harvard Business School Press, 1996), 33- 158.

to spend time with these people and encourage them. Under certain situations, they may appoint a team and charge them with helping to lead the church in setting priorities, recruiting help to plan goals and strategies for the coming year. Their influence and leadership can set the stage for changing the future direction of the congregation. They must spend time in prayer to hear from God.

Their influence and leadership can set the stage for changing the future direction of the congregation.

3. ***Develop a vision and strategy.*** Effective leaders are able to get a mental picture of what the church ought to do and be, and what it can be, and share that vision with the people. Going a step farther, they also have in mind beforehand the steps necessary to achieve the vision. This series of steps or accomplishments toward the final goal comprise the strategy. It is mentioned only briefly here, but it is the heart of the effort.

4. ***Communicate the change vision.*** As long as it remains locked up in leaders' hearts or in a written task-force report, the vision will not move the church forward. It must be communicated. How?

- In the pulpit in the context of biblically-grounded messages.
- In discussions in classes and small groups.
- Keep in mind that change frightens people. "Start low, go slow; rise higher, catch fire."

Little by little, line upon line, precept upon precept, people are willing to accept the vision if they have time to assimilate it and figure out their place in the new order of things. Further, church leaders can hold up as heroes those among them who are fulfilling Great Commission tasks. "Catch people doing something good and brag on them."

People are willing to accept the vision if they have time to assimilate it and figure out their place in the new order of things.

---

5. ***Empower broad-based action.*** A Great Commission congregation has many options for involvement of its people in evangelism, discipleship, and missions ministries. Good leaders will help their people find places in which ministries might be personally expressed on the basis of interest and spiritual giftedness. All the while, church leaders will hold up these examples of how individuals are acting to fulfill Christ's mandate. Every action taken and then spotlighted becomes a challenge to others to become involved in similar ministries. These can be as varied as

- local church visitation,
- evangelistic witnessing,
- acts of kindness,
- service in the community designed to win a hearing,
- mission trips to other countries,
- and more.

Experience has shown that each of these—and others—are within the reach of every size church.

6. ***Generate short-term wins.*** To change the direction and destination of a church is not the work of a moment. It doesn't happen in a week or two; it is a long-term process. But that is not to say that along the way, often early in the process, the church will not experience a "win" here and there. When that happens, church leaders need to make much of it.

- They can encourage testimonies by lay persons from the pulpit.
- They can interview a member in front of the congregation about involvement in a certain ministry and the sense of fulfillment that is felt when Christ is obeyed.
- They can use video testimonies.
- They can use bulletin inserts.

7. ***Consolidate gains and produce more change.*** Each success is a launching pad for the next step in moving toward being fully a Great Commission church. Each action gives an opportunity for it to be analyzed as to what went right and what can be improved, or what went wrong and might be avoided. "Yard by yard, everything's hard; inch by inch, life's a cinch!" Celebrate those who are moving toward achieving the vision.

8. ***Anchor new approaches in the church's culture.*** Once the changes are far enough along, they have essentially created a new culture for the congregation. No longer is the church existing or living for its own purposes, but it now measures its activities by asking how they relate to the Great Commission. The church can intentionally examine its schedule, calendar, budget, personnel assignments, based on

a Matthew 28 paradigm. Leaders can help the people of the church rejoice in their commitments to evangelism, discipleship, and missions and inspire them never to want to return to being a maintenance church.

Each success is a launching pad for the next step in moving toward being fully a Great Commission church.

To work effectively, this change strategy must be revisited often. Make a list of the eight steps and put it in a place where it will be seen frequently. Review its steps. Make it a part of weekly conversations. Keep it before church leaders.

Teaching the Congregation

Founding the preaching and teaching about Great Commission ministry solidly in Scripture and sound theology is absolutely necessary. Leaders should examine the Word and look at some theological underpinnings for helping the church adopt Christ's priorities.

1. *They must first be convinced that lost people are lost.* It is amazing in our Bible-saturated society, where every family owns two or three copies, that people are not convinced that unsaved people need Christ's redemption. One of the hallmarks of contemporary tolerant culture is that "all roads lead to God." If an individual is a Hindu or Buddhist or Muslim or a nonbeliever living in America, it doesn't much matter, according to this point of view. If a person's heart is good, God must certainly take that into consideration.

People must hear the gospel in order to be saved.

A beginning task of church leaders is to help people know the truth of the gospel: that Jesus is the way, the truth and the life and that no one comes to the Father except through Him. The church didn't originate this point of view; it came from the lips of Jesus himself (see John 14:6). This is so basic, believers often take for granted that everyone believes it; but not so. The gospel is the power of God unto salvation (Romans 1:16). There is salvation in no one else; "For there is no other name under heaven [that has been] given among men, by which we must be saved" (Acts 4:12).

People may try to couch it in more sophisticated language, but the truth is, hell is real, and it is the final destination of those who do not call on Jesus to be saved. Our people must be convinced of the lostness of humanity.

2. *People must hear the gospel in order to be saved.* Men and women who are not yet saved are held captive by Satan. Jesus came to plunder the Evil One's kingdom (Mark 3:27). He announced as His sacrificial death drew near, "Now judgment is upon this world; now the ruler of this world will be cast out. And I, if I am lifted up from the earth, will draw all men to Myself" (John 12:31, 32, *NASB*).

Paul's discussion in Romans 1 and 2 makes it clear that the wrath of God comes against the unrighteous. Unsaved people, wherever they are—in the United States or in the remotest part of the world—have an innate knowledge that there is a God, although that knowledge may be suppressed because of unrighteousness. They have a sense of right and wrong and they normally have a conscience that calls it to their attention when they do wrong. It is possible for the conscience to be darkened or seared, but it exists in men's hearts. People have a fear of death and whatever lies beyond it (Hebrews 2:14, 15). They are held captive by the Evil One until they are delivered by the power of the gospel. "If perhaps God may grant them repentance leading to the knowledge of the truth, and they may come to their senses and escape from the snare of the devil, having been held captive by him to do his will" (2 Timothy 2:25, 26, *NASB*).

In the great song of triumph of Romans 8, Christians are assured that they are on the winning side,

---

People must hear the gospel in order to be saved. "How shall they hear without a preacher? And how shall they preach unless they are sent" (Romans 10: 14, 15).

3. *Christians are in a war.* It is so easy in a culture that denies the existence or power of evil to understand that Christians are in a war against the dominion of Satan. One writer puts it clearly:

> *The Great Commission is a theology of cosmic warfare—a theology centering on the unveiling of the long-hidden mystery of Christ and His church. It means the overthrow of the ancient powers that have long held the creation captive through sin and death. It means the triumph of a resurrected Messiah over every principality and power hostile to the reign of the Creator. It*

> *means that God is keeping His promises to His anointed King. It means war.*[2]

In the Ephesians 6 passage about the believer's armor, Christians are told they can stand firm, they can resist, and they can extinguish the weapons aimed against them. In the great song of triumph of Romans 8, Christians are assured that they are on the winning side, that they will overwhelmingly conquer. This is the language of warfare.

In times of peace there is no readiness for battle, but if Christians recognize that they are in spiritual warfare, they will be ready to take their stand against the Enemy.

4. *Christians must be convinced of their ultimate triumph.* To see the apparent success of evil powers in the society around them and throughout the world is sometimes discouraging. One great truth that will provide reassurance and hope is that believers are on the winning side.

A young boy whose dad had put him in bed and told him to turn out the light was discovered using a little reading light and apparently talking to himself. The dad listened outside the door as his son was saying things like, "You don't know what I know!" and "Just you wait and see!" Looking into the room, the father saw that the boy was engrossed in a Tarzan adventure novel, chagrined that his dad had caught him still reading.

"It was so thrilling, Dad, that I couldn't stop reading! On every page it seemed Tarzan was going to be killed. His

---

2 Russell D. Moore, "A Theology of the Great Commission," in *The Challenge of the Great Commission* Chuck Lawless and Thom S. Rainer, eds., (Crestwood, Kentucky: Pinnacle Publishers, 2005), 50.

enemies were hot on his trail. I couldn't stand it, so I turned to the back and read the last chapter. Tarzan wins out!"

He had returned to his reading, but now he could say, "I've read the last chapter; I know how it all comes out."

Believers, too, have read the last chapter. The King of kings and Lord of lords is triumphant! He wins! And Christ-followers are on the winning side.

Great Commission Ministries

Faced with opportunities to put the Great Commission in the forefront of the church, leaders and members can ensure that they are fulfilling the Lord's instructions by participating in ministry on the local and the global scene.

Friendship Evangelism

Jimmy Long provides helpful insight into how a 21st-century conversion is likely to take place.[3] He describes it in terms of a six-step process, as follows:

1. Discontent with life
2. Confusion over meaning
3. Contact with Christians
4. Conversion to community
5. Commitment to Christ
6. Calling to heavenly vision

Friendship Evangelism, as it is described here, is a local church-centered strategy for reaching people and winning them to Christ.

---

3 Jimmy Long, *Generating Hope: A Strategy for Reaching the Postmodern Generation* (Downers Grove, Ill.: InterVarsity Press, 1997), 206-209.

Most everyone has acquaintances—relatives, coworkers, neighbors—who are unsaved and unchurched. Often believers are uninvolved in any effort that would move them toward the Lord or the church. This simple but effective evangelism ministry can be developed in any size church. It builds on the idea that evangelism is rarely an instantaneous event. It generally is a process that moves people from total noninvolvement with God and church to a place where they are vitally connected.

Little is accomplished if someone is challenged to accept Christ and remains unconnected with the body of Christ.

Another benefit of this particular approach is that it is church-centered. Little is accomplished if someone is challenged to accept Christ and remains unconnected with the body of Christ. Here's how Friendship Evangelism works.

1. ***Identifying spiritually needy people.*** The pastor invites the members of the congregation to survey their range of acquaintances with the goal of identifying two or three of them whose salvation they would like to see. Each member uses three 3x5 cards and writes the names—only the names—of the persons he or she is thinking about.

2. ***Seeking prayer support.*** Once the individuals have been identified, one card goes to the pastor, one is shared with a trusted brother or sister and the other is kept by the one who provided the names. These cards furnish the basis for concerted prayer for the salvation of each person named

on the card. At least three people are praying: (1) the friend who wrote the names, (2) a brother or sister invited to agree in prayer, and (3) the pastor.

3. ***Moving the friendship forward.*** Using a calendar, the person who has identified the two or three friends privately makes plans to intentionally spend time with those on his card in a several-month period. He thinks of activities the friend would like to do, and these can be extremely varied. What does the friend enjoy? Fishing, shopping, visiting flea markets, golfing, weight lifting, walking, biking, camping, going to athletic events, working on cars, dog training; it can be one or two of hundreds of activities.

The purpose of being with the friend is twofold: moving the friendship toward a deeper level of trust and showing the friend he or she is valued as a person.

The purpose of being with the friend is twofold: moving the friendship toward a deeper level of trust and showing the friend he or she is valued as a person. In the process, the nonbelievers come to see the Christian in daily life and observes a believer's lifestyle and—hopefully—joy.

4. ***Meeting other church people.*** During the period of weeks when personal friendships are being groomed, church leaders are planning for the church to sponsor activities that bring the church members together *outside the scope of regular church services.* What kinds of activities can go on the church calendar besides regular church services? Depending

on the time of year, it might be an all-church picnic; a youth-presented supper at church (perhaps in connection with a Youth World Evangelism Action fund-raising activity); a musical concert; church league athletic events; a Women's Ministry-sponsored yard sale; a homecoming "dinner on the grounds"; a Christmas drama; an Easter egg hunt; and on and on. Leaders are limited only by their imaginations as to the types of gatherings that might be envisioned in the life of the church.

The purpose of the nonservice activities is to give a venue for inviting a friend into the circle of the church in a non-threatening setting. He is invited to come along with his sponsoring friend and may be introduced to a few of the church members. This helps him feel at ease in the church community.

5. ***Moving into the sanctuary.*** At an appropriate time when the friends have spent time with each other and the friend has become acquainted with some of the church people, it is the suitable moment for an invitation to a sanctuary experience. This might be a regular church service, a special seasonal event, or even (though not in the sanctuary) a small group gathering.

Although 90 percent of Americans say they believe in God, only about 17 percent of them are in church on a given Sunday.

The purpose here is to allow the friends to experience church as it is practiced. They will hear the music and engage with the sermon or lesson. Why is this necessary? Because although 90 percent of Americans say they believe in God, only about 17 percent of them are in church on a given Sunday. Gallup's research indicates that nearly half the population has not been exposed to any religious training during their upbringing.[4] To those of us who grew up in church or have been attending for any length of time, it is almost inconceivable that anyone in America has not experienced church, but that's the reality in which we live.

6. ***Presenting an invitation to follow Christ.*** Not every pastor in every service gives the plan of salvation and an opportunity to pray, so arranging for the friend to hear a presentation of God's provision for salvation requires a bit of collusion with the pastor. Once it is known that the friend will be present, the pastor can make appropriate plans for the sermon and the closing.

The purpose of the gospel presentation is to make clear to the nonbeliever that he needs salvation and salvation has been provided.

A young salesman being trained under an older, experienced practitioner attempted to move the buyer to a decision and failed in the attempt. Talking to his mentor later, he said "You can lead a horse to water, but you can't make him drink." To which the older salesman pointed out, "It's not your job to make him drink; it's your job to convince him he is thirsty!"

---

[4] Reported by George G. Hunter III, Distinguished Professor of Church Growth and Evangelism at Asbury Theological Seminary, in an address to Church of God leaders in Cleveland, Tennessee.

The pastor's challenge is to help people realize they need redemption and that it is available.

7. ***Staying connected.*** What a joy to see a friend come to know Christ! That is the beginning of discipleship. In Chapter 3 of this book, I've discussed this vital ministry; the point here is that the job is not done until the new believer has been incorporated into the life of the church. The friend's work is unfinished until he uses his encouragement to move the baby Christian into a discipling environment.

Friendship Evangelism is only one way of winning people to Christ. It may not be the best way, but it has the advantage of being nonthreatening and natural. It does not demand a mastery of soulwinning techniques or years of experience as an evangelist.

Some years ago a celebration was held at the end of summer at a New Orleans municipal pool. The party around the pool celebrated the first summer in memory without a drowning at any of the city's public pools. In honor of the occasion, 200 people gathered, including 100 certified lifeguards. As the party was breaking up and the four lifeguards on duty began to clear the pool, they found a fully-dressed body in the deep end. They tried to revive Jerome Moody, 31, but it was too late. He had drowned surrounded by lifeguards celebrating their successful season.

The church can have a plethora of activities in progress, but unless they zero in on the Great Commission—connecting, converting, discipling, equipping, and empowering—they miss the point.

Regardless of the method that is used, the important goal is helping people come into a right relationship with Christ and a connection to His church.

> ***For useful forms and further instructions about Friendship Evangelism and for links to other recommended evangelism ideas, visit* www.greatcommission.cc.**

Church Planting

Jesus said, "I will build my church" (Matthew 16:18). Paul, reflecting on the development of the local church in Corinth, wrote: "I planted, Apollos watered, but God gave the increase . . . For we are God's fellow workers" (1 Corinthians 3:6, 9).

The establishment of a new church is the product of God's working by His Spirit through His servants. It is clearly the church as an instrument and an end that Christ had in mind when He gave the Great Commission. The Book of Acts witnesses the Commission in action. It is the church that sends church planters (Acts 13:1-3). It is by their activity that converts are won, and it is new churches that result from their going (Acts 14:23). It is in the context of the church that teaching takes place (Acts 11:23). Against the background of the successful church-planting ministry recorded in Acts, it is easy to understand the observation made by Donald A. McGavran, father of the Church Growth movement,

> *Any discipling of the peoples of the earth, of all the peoples of the earth, necessitates aiming at establishing millions of new congregations. Carrying out the world mission of the Church is impossible, it is empty words, unless it rides on the back of mul-*

> *titudes of new congregations of the redeemed spreading through every ethnic and linguistic unit of mankind.*[5]

Churches today know they must make careful distinctions between the cultures of the New Testament and the societies in which they live and work in the 21st century, but they may consider the patterns of church planting in the Book of Acts as models from which they can learn.

1. ***A preacher and a team.*** The church in Jerusalem was born out of the pyrotechnics of Pentecost. However, the most that may be said for the strange events that attracted a crowd after the unusual witness of the Holy Spirit in the Upper Room is that the people were awestruck and astounded. No significant movement toward God happened—and no new church was begun—until the Word of God was preached and the people responded in faith.

The founding group of this church was men and women who had prepared for the event by praying, fasting, and waiting for the Holy Spirit. The fact that people from 16 languages and dialects heard the gospel is a testimony that the church is a community that can bring healing to the divisions of humankind. Church planters have learned the truth that people are more prone to gather with those who are like them. The only commonality of the Day of Pentecost gathering was that they were in the city to celebrate Pentecost. God worked through His Word and Spirit to reach them.

The preaching was both contemporary and biblical, a fact that should not be lost on church planters who want to

---

[5] Donald A. McGavran, "Try These Seven Steps for Planting Churches," *Global Church Growth Bulletin, 18,* May-June 1981, 18.

faithfully communicate the gospel and relate to their audience. James Stewart, a great Scottish preacher in Aberdeen, once observed, "Every sermon must begin in Aberdeen and end in Jerusalem, or else begin in Jerusalem and end in Aberdeen." He was saying, of course, that a sermon must be biblical (Jerusalem) and must relate to where the hearers live (Aberdeen). Peter started his sermon by referring to recent events in Jerusalem, then moved to quote passages from the Old Testament.

Peter was not a solo act. "But Peter, standing up with the eleven, raised his voice" (Acts 2:14). He was the preacher, but he was part of a team. Teams demonstrate the communal nature of the church. Teams provide courage. Teams produce a prayer base. Teams give evidence that a newcomer will have a group of friends with whom to associate. The result of the Pentecost experience was unique and groundbreaking. Following the testimonies of the 120 Spirit-inspired disciples and the team-backed efforts of Peter, fully 3,000 new converts came into the Kingdom, and the church in Jerusalem was born.

2. ***A geographical move.*** The church that was established in Antioch (Acts 11:19-30) came about as the result of the witness of Christians who had moved there from Jerusalem. To their surprise, non-Jewish people gladly responded to the gospel. At times, church planters may be summoned to a location where a nucleus of believers has already gathered; this was evidently the case in Antioch. Barnabas, the Encourager, became leader of the group, but he quickly discerned the necessity of in-depth instruction for the believers.

He traveled to Tarsus to find Paul and bring him as a teacher who would help the believers become founded in the Word. One of the vital needs of a new church, especially one constituted primarily of new converts, is thorough and insightful instruction.

3. ***Following a vision.*** The church planters had no plans to start a church in Philippi until God divinely intervened by means of a vision of a man of the city who appeared to Paul and asked him to come and help (Acts 16:9). The foundation of the church at Philippi was thus sovereignly directed by God. It is not unusual for a church planter to testify that God has placed a particular burden on his heart to start a church in a certain place.

The effort in Philippi was aided considerably by a wealthy woman named Lydia, who embraced the message of the gospel at first hearing and offered her home as a haven for the church planters. As often happens today, God prepares the hearts of key individuals in connection with the establishment of a new church, and they become stalwart supporters of the effort. An unusual assortment of such people in Philippi—a rich businesswoman, a formerly demon-possessed girl and a converted jail keeper—were among the people God signaled to help with church planting.

4. ***Teaching as evangelism.*** The founding of the church in Corinth (Acts 18) models two primary lessons for church pioneers. The first lesson is, church planters should approach their task in the full confidence that God goes before them and prepares the hearts of people for whom the gospel message is destined: "Do not be afraid, but speak, and do not

keep silent; for I am with you, and no one will attack you to hurt you; for I have many people in this city" (Acts 18:9, 10) became a word of encouragement for the apostle. The understanding that Christ is building His church and that He already knows people in the city where the new church is being planted—even before they are converted—who are potential members should provide encouragement and comfort for today's modern apostles.

The second lesson is, part of Paul's success lay in his ability to interact with people with religious opinions in a way that brought them to Christ. He used teaching as an evangelistic tool. Church planters can use teaching to gain and ground their converts.

5. ***Contemporary mother-daughter church planting.*** One of the most successful models of church planting in contemporary North America is what is termed the "mother-daughter" method. God moves on the heart of church leaders to help ensure the success of a daughter church.

In these cases, the daughter might be near—in the same town or a nearby town—or distant. The mother church sends and supports the church planter and provides resources that are helpful. The pastor of the mother church becomes a mentor to the church-planting pastor. Close contact is maintained, and at times, members of the mother church go temporarily or permanently to provide a foundation on which the young congregation grows. Many of the Church of God's most effective church plants follow the mother-daughter model.

One further important point must be made: Church leaders must open their hearts to the importance of church planting. I can't tell you how often I have heard of church leaders who are gung-ho for new churches to be planted—as long as it happens somewhere else.

I preached some months ago in Indonesia at a large Gereja Bethel (Church of God) church in a Jakarta suburb, conducting two Sunday morning services. Hundreds attended the services. When we ended the service and started to drive away, my guide pointed out another Gereja Bethel congregation almost across the street.

World Missions

Every local church in the Church of God can be a Great Commission church, fulfilling the clear and implicit instructions of the Lord to "go into all the world." Thanks to a well-administered World Missions ministry operating out of Cleveland, Tennessee, whose stated goal is "to help local churches fulfill their Great Commission calling," local churches have numerous opportunities.

1. ***Go as missionaries.*** Dozens of people each year apply and are accepted to go to other countries and cultures as missionaries. World Missions offers publications and instructions for those who feel a calling in this area. Six different categories of missionaries serve the church and the Lord, and there seems always to be a need for more people who will respond. World Missions sends

- Bible school teachers
- Medical personnel
- Orphanage directors
- Construction personnel

- Vocational training personnel

2. ***Sponsor missionaries.*** "How shall they preach unless they are sent?" asks Romans 10:15. Each year numerous missionaries return from the field and visit churches in order to secure financial partners. They invite individuals, Sunday school classes, and local churches to commit to a definite amount each month that will enable them to stay on the field.

First Samuel 30 tells the story of David's successful pursuit of enemies who had attacked and devastated his town. Only part of his force accompanied him into the heat of the chase and battle; another part had remained back in the town. But when they returned with the spoils of battle, David announced that all of them would share in the fruit of victory. "For as his share is who goes down to the battle, so shall his share be who stays by the baggage; they shall share alike" (1 Samuel 30:24, *NASB*).

The missionary who goes and the giver who makes it possible for her to go will share alike in the rewards of Christ!

3. ***Adopt a project.*** The Church of God ministers in 179 countries around the world, and ministry often takes place among poor people. When they need church buildings or Bible schools or orphanages, they are usually unable to pay all the costs. Local churches in the United States have discovered the joy of partnering with the church in other countries in completing their projects.

Only on rare occasions does a donor church pay all the costs of a project. Typically, the national church raises all the money it can and provides all the labor it can, but help is needed. Projects are partnerships. They may vary from as little as a few hundred dollars to extremely large amounts. In a recent report, I saw project requests that asked for $250 all the way up to one that amounted to $300,000 from one church over a period of time. Project lists are available from World Missions, and donors may wish to inquire about projects in a certain geographical area, or in a certain amount, or by the type of project (church, school, orphanage, water well, Bibles, boat, motorcycle, and so forth.)

4. ***Take a trip.*** It is difficult to get the picture of needs on the mission field from the comfort of a home or office. World Missions offers numerous opportunities for people to travel to overseas destinations for ministry or assistance. Teams from *Men and Women of Action*—made up of volunteer laymen who are carpenters, masons, electricians, plumbers, roofers, or just laborers—go many times a year for a week or two weeks and participate in building projects. They are always seeking team members.

Groups from *People for Care and Learning* go frequently to Southeast Asia for ministry purposes. This organization, governed by a board appointed by World Missions, is a standalone, non-governmental agency that operates orphanages, provides vocational training, teaches English and engages in other work in countries that do not traditionally admit Christian missionaries.

Approved evangelists abroad, volunteer pastors and evangelists who have been approved by World Missions, go to conduct evangelistic crusades and always desire to have team members accompany them. *STEP* trips made up of teens and college-age students schedule ministry travel.

These and other opportunities are available to pastors and church members who want to experience front-line Great Commission ministry.

5. ***Pray.*** Most missionaries recruit men and women, boys and girls, who will covenant to keep them in prayer. A spiritual battle rages when the ambassadors of the King perform their work, and they need a battalion of pray-ers holding them up in prayer.

Finally

The next time the circus comes to your town, go. Study the lions and the lion tamer. He will have a whip, a pistol and a chair. Don't think for a minute the lions are afraid of the whip or pistol. (Are you kidding, a *scared* lion?) The lions respond because of the chair.

You see, a lion is a carnivorous hunter. He focuses on his prey with single vision. Without vision he cannot attack or charge his prey. He tries to focus on the chair, but the four legs confuse his sense of visual acuity. Animal trainers say the lion is mesmerized by trying to focus on all four chair legs at the same time.

The reason for this book is for you to focus on one thing: The Great Commission. You cannot do everything. But you can do one thing: Live a Great Commission life.

If you have read this far, you are probably serious about your assigned mission to your piece of the world, your "dispensation of the gospel." I have written about connecting, converting, discipling, equipping, and empowering. That's pretty simple strategy. Now, here's some advice.

1. Don't be mesmerized with all the baggage of a post-modern world. Sure, the church is in transition. But it has always been in some sort of transition. Just be conversant with your context and your culture, and you will do well.
2. Don't become confused with all the hot talk about seeker, emergent, mosaic, or cutting-edge churches. *Being* church is much more important than *doing* church. We know how to "do" church; our problem is "being" the church.
3. Don't fall for fads (an acrostic that stands for "For a day"). It is another way of saying, "Here today and gone tomorrow."

After a lifetime of observing a changing world and church, I am convinced of these three things:

- **People need Jesus Christ.**
- **Jesus Christ needs missionaries.**
- **The Great Commission is the solution to both.**

Too simple?

It is, if you like to do things that are tension-relieving and not Kingdom achieving.

It is, if you like fighting battles when you gain no ground by winning.

It is, if success means more to you than surrender, service, and sacrifice.

Don't hear what I'm *not* saying. I'm not saying simple is easy, or quick, or popular. Jesus must have understood how difficult His simple strategy would be.

The next time you look around at your world and wonder why He doesn't do something—remember, He did.

He made you.

Solution Points

1. Identify a pastor in your area who is easily recognized as a Great Commission pastor. Arrange a conversation with him or her and ask how he/she became motivated for this type of ministry involvement.
2. Consider the concept of spiritual authority. Can it be abused? How?
3. Develop a change plan for your church using the steps outlined by Kotter. Do this in concert with a few of the key leaders in the congregation. Listen to their advice and counsel as you attempt to foresee opportunities and opposition. Think in these terms: "X-months from now, I want our church to be like this."
4. Outline a lesson or sermon on this subject: "People Outside of Christ Are Truly Lost."
5. Recruit a core group from the congregation who will help develop a Friendship Evangelism ministry during the coming six months.
6. Survey the geographical area within reach of your church with the goal of helping to plant a church, perhaps in concert with other churches, as a "mother church."
7. Work with the pastor to get a Local Church Mission Representative out of your congregation. Visit the Church of God World Missions Web site (*www.cogwm.org*) to learn how a Local Mission Representative (LMR) can help.
8. Study opportunities for involvement in World Missions (their Web site can offer lots of help) and select a way of connecting with Missions during the coming year.

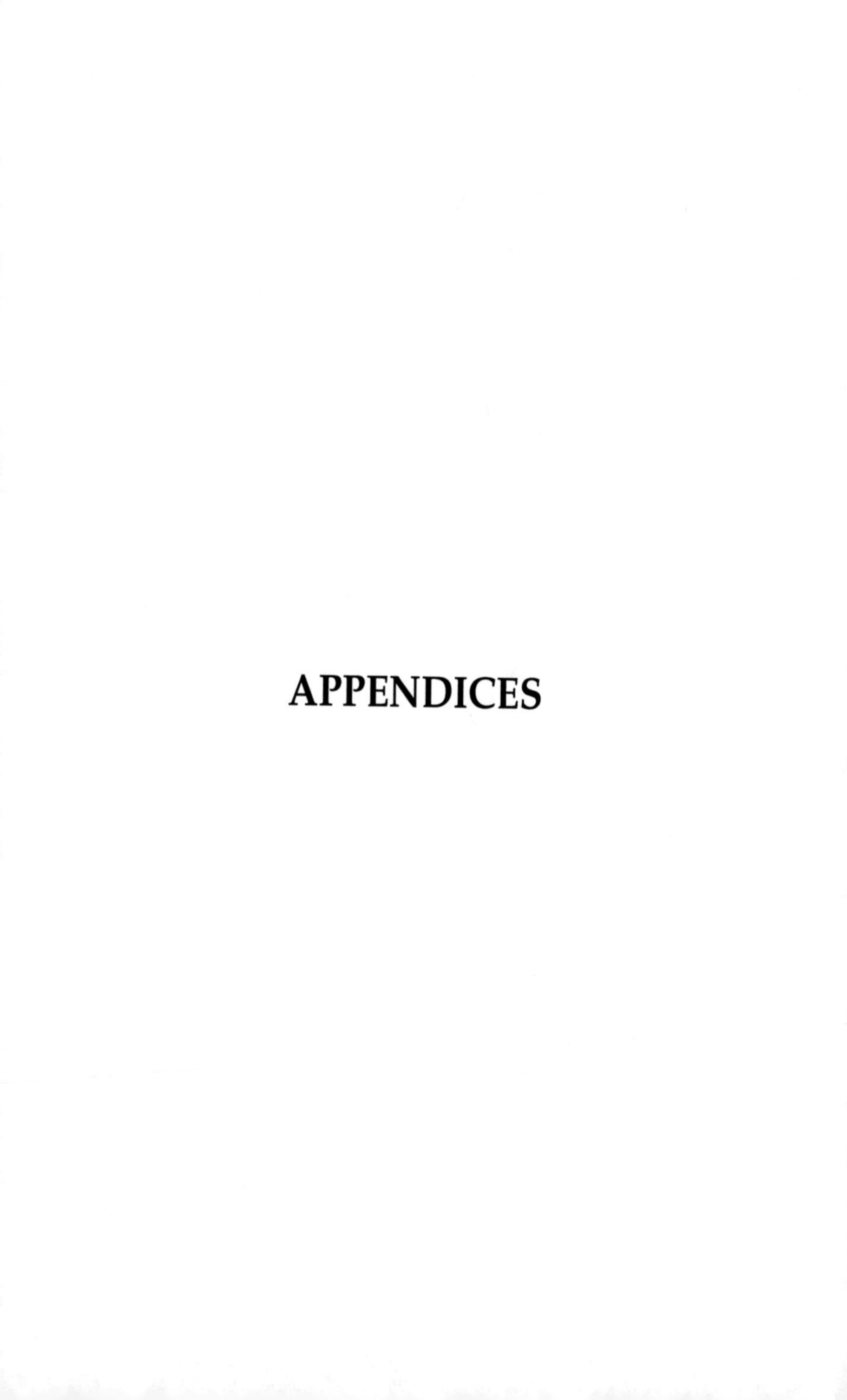

APPENDICES

Appendix A

Discover Your Grace Gift(s)[1]

A Self-Discovery Survey

This survey is designed to help Christians discern their grace gift. It is not a fool-proof method, however, it should provide a guideline to help you discover your gift. For some who take this survey, your spiritual gift will become obvious. For others, it will help to narrow down your gift to two or three of the most likely possibilities. By using additional input, you should be able to further discern your spiritual gift.

Little value will be derived from using this survey unless it is accompanied with studying the biblical teachings on spiritual gifts. This survey is developed to be used as one part of a total study on spiritual gifts.

Survey Instructions

1. Write your response to each statement on the answer sheet.
2. Please respond to every statement. Do not leave any statement blank.
3. Respond to each statement by placing one of the following numbers in the appropriate box:
   - 2 = If the statement always or almost always characterizes you
   - 1 = If the statement sometimes characterizes you
   - 0 = If the statement rarely characterizes you

Scoring Instructions

1. After you have completed the survey, add the total of each column (A through G) and write this number on the appropriate line at the bottom of the column. This is your raw score.

---

1 The Spiritual Gifts Survey and the Spiritual Passion Assessment were developed by Dr. Michael Chapman, pastor of City Church, Chattanooga, Tennessee.

2. Enter each raw score under the appropriate column on the Gift Graph.
3. Using the Conversion of Raw Score to Percentile Score table, determine your percentile score. Enter your percentile score on the graph. (For example: A raw score of 23 would convert to a percentile score of 77.)
4. Plot the percentile scores on the graph and draw a line between the dots.

Spiritual Gift Survey

2 = always **1 = sometimes** **0 = rarely**

1. I have a strong hatred for sin and grieve when I see it in my life or in the lives of other people.
2. I like to work on short-term rather than long-term projects.
3. I check out the facts carefully before I believe what I hear.
4. I enjoy counseling people.
5. I have the ability to make wise purchases and investments.
6. I have the ability to see the overall picture and clarify long-range goals.
7. I am an extremely loving and kind person.
8. I speak frankly and boldly to a person when I sense a spiritual lack in his/her life.
9. I have the ability to recall the specific likes and dislikes of people.
10. I really get upset when someone uses a scripture out of context.
11. I enjoy talking to troubled, discouraged people to encourage them to live victoriously.
12. I like to give anonymously.
13. I enjoy delegating tasks and supervising people.

14. I quickly sense when a person is troubled about something.
15. I have the ability to discern the character and motives of people.
16. I am alert to detect and meet practical needs.
17. I am more interested in facts than opinions.
18. I believe that all teaching must have some practical application.
19. I like to feel a part of the ministries to which I contribute.
20. I like to accomplish tasks as quickly and efficiently as possible.
21. I am drawn to hurting people.
22. I set very high standards for myself because I desire to live strictly by biblical standards.
23. I like to keep things in meticulous order.
24. I love to study and do research.
25. I see people's problems as stepping stones to victory in their lives.
26. I do not respond to emotional appeals. I give only as led by the Holy Spirit.
27. I have an awareness of resources available to complete a task.
28. I have a desire to remove hurts and bring healing to others.
29. I am very frank and outspoken, I usually do not mince words
30. I would rather be a helper than a leader.
31. I like to present truth in a logical, systematic way.
32. I have a very positive mental attitude. I am an optimist.
33. I am a good financial manager.

34. I like clear lines of authority and responsibility.
35. I use firmness with people only as a last resort.
36. I have a deep concern for the reputation and program of God
37. I have the desire to sense sincere appreciation and the ability to detect insincerity.
38. When teaching, I emphasize the accuracy of the point I am making more than how people can apply the truth to their lives.
39. I really like working with people.
40. I love to give freely of my money, time and talents.
41. I consider myself a visionary person.
42. I have a sensitivity to words and actions that hurt other people.
43. I want others to point out the blind spots in my life.
44. I am happiest when doing something helpful for someone.
45. I particularly enjoy doing word studies.
46. I easily accept people as they are without judging them.
47. I enjoy meeting needs without the pressure of appeals.
48. I am the happiest when working toward the accomplishment of specific goals.
49. I always look for the good in other people.
50. I have very strong opinions on most subjects and almost always verbalize them.
51. I love to entertain people in my home.
52. I like following established sources of truth.
53. I enjoy working with people who are eager to follow steps of action.

54. I am definitely not gullible.
55. I am more task-oriented than people-oriented.
56. I easily sense the spiritual or emotional mood of a person or group.
57. I feel a strong call to intercessory prayer.
58. I get frustrated when limitations of time are placed on a project.
59. I feel Bible study is foundational to all the gifts.
60. When someone has a problem, I love to give specific steps of action that will help move him out of the trial.
61. I am hard working and usually successful at what I do.
62. I am very enthusiastic about whatever I am involved.
63. I think it is very important to be sensitive to people's feelings.
64. To me, people and situations are either in the will of God or out of the will of God-there is no in between.
65. I tend to do more than I am asked to do.
66. I check out the knowledge source of other teachers.
67. When I have a problem in a relationship, I go to the other person right away to straighten it out.
68. I give high-quality gifts.
69. I really like to organize events and projects.
70. I often find myself serving as a mediator between people with troubled or broken relationships.
71. I would rather give a speech (sermon, lesson lecture, etc.) than do the research for the speech.
72. I am energetic with a high energy level.
73. I am slow in accepting the viewpoint of others.

74. I like to think out loud when trying to analyze something.
75. I strongly believe that everything belongs to God and I am just a channel.
76. I can endure criticism in order to get the job done.
77. I do not cope well with conflict or confrontation.
78. I would rather speak before a large group than to an individual.
79. I would rather do a job myself than delegate it to others.
80. I would rather help people by teaching a class than by personal counseling.
81. I can form my ideas better when I dialogue with someone rather than just analyzing things myself.
82. I enjoy giving what meets the practical needs of others.
83. I get great fulfillment in seeing pieces fit together and others enjoying the finished product.
84. I seem to have an inner instinct about things.
85. I enjoy research primarily to clarify and prove what I have presented.
86. I tend to be a perfectionist.
87. I would rather teach a class than be involved in personal witnessing.
88. I am a good verbal communicator.
89. I view hospitality as an opportunity to give.
90. I desire to move on to a new challenge when a previous one is completed.
91. I am ruled more by my heart than by my head.
92. When speaking before a group, I feel it is important to see an immediate response of commitment.

93. I would rather help someone by meeting a specific need than by teaching him how to provide for himself.
94. Reading is one of my hobbies.
95. I become frustrated when someone teaches without clear practical application.
96. I would rather function supportively in the background than speak in front of a group.
97. I like to plan ahead rather than take things as they come.
98. It is more important to me that everyone is happy rather than everything is done exactly right.
99. I would rather spend time in prayer and fasting than organizing a Christian project.
100. I find it hard to say no when asked to help with a project.
101. When faced with a problem, I start by looking at God's Word.
102. I like to read how to books.
103. I quickly volunteer to help when I see a need.
104. I really enjoy designing steps that help solve a problem.
105. Sometimes it is difficult for me to be decisive.

Answer Sheet

2 = always **1 = sometimes** **0 = rarely**

A	B	C	D	E	F	G
1	2	3	4	5	6	7
8	9	10	11	12	13	14
15	16	17	18	19	20	21
22	23	24	25	26	27	28
29	30	31	32	33	34	35
36	37	38	39	40	41	42
43	44	45	46	47	48	49
50	51	52	53	54	55	56
57	58	59	60	61	62	63
64	65	66	67	68	69	70
71	72	73	74	75	76	77
78	79	80	81	82	83	84
85	86	87	88	89	90	91
92	93	94	95	96	97	98
99	100	101	102	103	104	105

	A	B	C	D	E	F	G
Raw Score Total							

Conversion of Raw Score to Percentile Score

Raw Score	1	2	3	4	5	6	7	8	9	10	11	12	13	14	15
Percentile	3	7	10	13	17	20	23	27	30	33	37	40	43	47	50
Raw Score	16	17	18	19	20	21	22	23	24	25	26	27	28	29	30
Percentile	53	57	60	63	67	70	73	77	80	83	87	90	93	97	100

Gift Graph

	A Prophesying	B Serving	C Teaching	D Encouraging	E Giving	F Ruling	G Showing Mercy
Raw Score							
Percentile							
100	•	•	•	•	•	•	•
95	•	•	•	•	•	•	•
90	•	•	•	•	•	•	•
85	•	•	•	•	•	•	•
80	•	•	•	•	•	•	•
75	•	•	•	•	•	•	•
70	•	•	•	•	•	•	•
65	•	•	•	•	•	•	•
60	•	•	•	•	•	•	•
55	•	•	•	•	•	•	•
50	•	•	•	•	•	•	•
45	•	•	•	•	•	•	•
40	•	•	•	•	•	•	•
35	•	•	•	•	•	•	•
30	•	•	•	•	•	•	•
25	•	•	•	•	•	•	•
20	•	•	•	•	•	•	•
15	•	•	•	•	•	•	•
10	•	•	•	•	•	•	•
5	•	•	•	•	•	•	•

Appendix B

Spiritual Passion Assessment

In each of the six boxes, there is a question. You must choose among the five responses to each question which would be your most and which would be your least positive response to the question.

Least	If you had the opportunity to attend a major conference, which of the following would you most like to attend and which would you least like to attend?	Most
	SC A conference on the historical development of Christian doctrine	
	H A conference on how to help people who are struggling with grief	
	A A conference on soul winning	
	S A worship conference	
	F A conference on hospitality ministry	

Least	You have decided to give a week of your vacation and volunteer to do something for God's Kingdom. Where would you most likely give your time? Where would you least likely give your time?	Most
	SC The Christian Education ministry of your church	
	A Go on a missioins trip	
	H The women's shelter your church helps support	
	S The worship department of the church	
	F Landscaping and outdoor beautification project of the church	

Least	Your church is looking for volunteers in a variety of ministries. Which of the following would you most like to volunteer for and which you least like to volunteer for?	Most
	A The Intercessory Prayer Group	
	H Support Group ministry for people struggling with addictions	
	SC Young Adult Sunday School Class	
	S Sanctuary Choir	
	F The set-up crew	

Least	You have an extra $100 to spend on books. Which resources would you most likely purchase and which would you least likely purchase?	Most
	S Most recent worship music from your favorite worship leader	
	SC A set of discipleship studies that you would like to use to lead a group	
	H A set of books on people helping skills from the American Association of Christian Counselors	
	F A Christian Education Course on the spiritual formation of children	
	A A set of books on the moral decline of modern society	

Least	Which topic would you be more likely to stay up late discussing with a group of friends and which would you be least likely to stay up late discussing?	Most
	H How to start a lay counseling ministry at your church	
	F How to begin a monthly fellowship program for the senior members of your church	
	A How to stop the spread of pornography in your community	
	S How to increase the size of the church choir	
	SC How to develop a teacher training program for your adult teachers	

Least	If you had $5,000 that you could donate to a ministry that is close to your heart, where would you most likely donate it and where would you least likely donate it? (assume that there is a need for each of these things at your church)	Most
	SC Purchase new lighting and video equipment for the worship center.	
	F Pay to redecorate the church foyer and develop a welcome center	
	A Build a church on the mission field.	
	SC Purchase new teaching resources	
	H Give it to needy families.	
	S The worship department of the church	
	F Landscaping and outdoor beautification project of the church	

1. In column one, add the number of most responses for each of the statements designated as S, A, H, SC, and F and enter the number in the appropriate boxes. The total number of most responses must equal 6. If it does not, please refigure your most responses.

2. In column two, add the number of least responses for each of the statements designated as S, A, H, SC, and F and enter the number in the appropriate boxes. The total number of least responses must equal 6. If it does not, please refigure your least responses.

3. Subtract column two (least) from column one (most) and enter that number in column three. This number may be a negative number.

4. Plot your score for each of the five spiritual passions on the graph, connecting the points to form a line graph.

Most	Least	Difference
S	S	S
A	A	A
H	H	H
SC	SC	SC
F	F	F
Total must = 6	Total must = 6	

	S **Sanctuary**	**A** **Army**	**H** **Hospital**	**SC** **School**	**F** **Family**
6					
5					
4					
3					
2					
1					
0					
-1					
-2					
-3					
-4					
-5					
-6